I0500121

THE FOURTEENTH AMENDMENT IN ITS INTENT FOR EDUCATION

And Their Words Come Tripping After

Robert Stuart

© 2017 Robert Stuart
All rights reserved.

ISBN: 1548164909
ISBN 13: 9781548164904
Library of Congress Control Number: 2017909848
CreateSpace Independent Publishing Platform
North Charleston, South Carolina

The Fourteenth Amendment In Its Intent for Education

And Their Words Come Tripping After.

This publication is a reprint of my 1960 M.A. thesis from the University of Wisconsin. The title of the thesis is, "The Intent of the Framers of the Fourteenth Amendment Concerning the Question of Separate Negro Schools."

I entered the University of Wisconsin as a graduate student in the fall term, 1956. I had been graduated the previous June from DePauw University with a major in history and had been awarded the Albert J. Beveridge Fellowship from DePauw for graduate study at Wisconsin.

My graduate professor was Howard K. Beale, who in consultation with me for a thesis asked if I would undertake a study of the Fourteenth Amendment in relation to the intent of the framers of that Amendment with regard to the question of separate or integrated schools.

As a Reconstruction historian professor Beale had a pointed interest. He had been among several historians who were asked to provide historical background for Brown v. The Board of Education of Topeka, which in 1954 led to the Supreme Court decision in support of integration. The decision overturned the "separate but equal" decision of the Supreme Court in Plessy v. Ferguson, 1896. Both cases relied on interpretation of the Fourteenth Amendment.

In proposing a more exhaustive study of the question historically, Beale told me that he felt he had been rushed to provide accurate historical background for the Brown case. It wasn't that he disagreed with the decision but that he felt the subject had not yet been thoroughly researched.

C. Van Woodward was a PhD student under Beale at the University of North Carolina when Beale had taught there. Van Woodward had in 1955 just published *The Strange Career of Jim Crow*, which showed by research that, contrary to what may have been assumed, Jim Crow laws did not become an established pattern of segregation until the 1890s. Prior to that time, practices among the states varied. Beale therefore wondered in conversation with me what a more thoroughly researched study on the subject of the Fourteenth Amendment and Negro education might reveal. Or more pointedly, what may have been the stated or perceived intent of that Amendment relative to schools in the education of those now free because of the abolition of slavery by the Thirteenth Amendment? The research focused on debates in Congress, ratification among the states, statements from departments of education, and comment in the press, 1866 to the Civil Rights Act of 1875.

The resulting research for me, and the writing of the thesis, was thorough and exhaustive. Beale would have it no other way. He kept me at it through several revisions. Having completed my course work for my degree but not yet having completed the thesis to Beale's satisfaction, I was drafted and served as a conscientious objector working at the University of Kansas Medical Center, 1958-1959. During that time I continued to write drafts of chapters of the thesis, sending them to Beale. For personal reasons I decided in 1959 to enter Princeton Theological Seminary. My thesis was complete, though Beale had not signed off on it, and we were in continuing correspondence about that. Then in December 1959 he died unexpectedly of a heart attack. Beale's students were assigned to other professors by a committee from the history department. Since my work was complete, a date was set for my oral exam for my degree. I met with the committee, which included Merle Curti, and I was then recommended to receive my degree. The M.A. degree was awarded in the spring term, 1960.

I have always felt the subject of the thesis remained current, augmented by more recent interest in Reconstruction history. I note here that use of the word "doctrine" as in separate but equal doctrine is to be identified with its formalization in Plessy v. Fergeson in 1896. Prior to that time, while the concept was there and so stated, policies and practice were fluid among the states.

In more personal comment, research from my time as a student was all by hand, taking notes in writing from the primary sources. Anyone from the same time will appreciate that. It was for me a time to be buried in the stacks of the University of Wisconsin Library and other repositories. The smell of old pages, the room temperatures and humidity, the ink at the fingertips, all are tactile remembrances. There was also at times a sense of historical dislocation. Thus once in writing a letter to a friend, I dated it 1858. Then there was the typing up of notes on a manual typewriter, for me the Smith Corona I had taken to college at DePauw. The work of a thesis or dissertation took time. There was no instant screen time. What we had were the remains from the day, the print records of their time.

There is for me an appreciation of that process and for the rigors of such work. Beale in seminars with his graduate students was a bear, though a patrician one. My first time to present a paper was a rite of passage. All of us as graduate students were sharp edged, ready to get at weaknesses in another's presentation. No holds barred. After the other students had been at me for some time in my first reading and defense, Mr. Beale having sat back while the spectacle carried on as though an arena, he eventually leaned forward, his hands across the vest of his suit, and said, "All right, gentlemen, I think we've had enough of Mr. Stuart today."

To be in Beale's seminar was to think critically or get out. He was a taskmaster also in skills of writing, rhetoric and syntax as well as basic rules of grammar and spelling. Fortunately I had not come to his seminar unprepared, because such skills in thinking and writing were important at DePauw and before that in high school at Webster Groves, Missouri. But I was relieved to have successfully run the gauntlet that first time out. I continued thereafter with confidence. And perseverance.

Robert B. Stuart
2017

THE INTENT OF THE FRAMERS OF THE FOURTEENTH
AMENDMENT CONCERNING THE QUESTION OF
SEPARATE NEGRO SCHOOLS
BY
ROBERT BEECHER STUART

A thesis submitted in partial fulfillment of the
requirements for the degree of

MASTER OF ARTS
(History)
at the
UNIVERSITY OF WISCONSIN

1960

Respectfully Dedicated
to
Professor Howard K. Beale
who, in his life, guided the work of this thesis,
and who remains an example for
sound and thorough research

INTRODUCTION

The question to which this paper seeks an answer is the intent of the framers of the Fourteenth Amendment concerning Negro education. Was it their intent to include education within the Amendment's guarantee of civil equality? If this was their intent, did they believe the Amendment called for integration? Or did they feel the segregation issue outside the scope of the Amendment? Finally, what was thought to be the change caused by the Amendment in the balance of power between state and federal authority?

The broadest possible scope has been given to the word "framers" in order to gain the most accurate concept of what was thought between 1866 and 1868 to be the meaning of section one of the Fourteenth Amendment as a guarantee of civil equality. "Framers" thus includes both the Congress that passed the Amendment and the states that ratified it.

This study goes beyond the Thirty-ninth Congress, which produced the Amendment, however. The guarantee of civil equality occupied congressional attention until March 1, 1875, when the last of the civil rights bills was signed by President Grant. The civil rights debate between 1872 and 1875 is particularly significant because there were lengthy discussions about the meaning of the Amendment with regard to the school segregation issue, and because some of the members of the Thirty-ninth Congress were still in Congress at the time. This study therefore includes the ten year period, 1866-1875.

The same period of time is taken for the states to determine, first, their immediate reaction to the Amendment when considering its ratification and, second, their attitudes toward the Negro during these ten years. Did state legislation and did policies and practices within the departments of education, in other words, reflect the opinion that the Fourteenth Amendment embodied a definition of civil equality that included, either Negro education per se or integration in the schools?

TABLE OF CONTENTS

CHAPTER 1

CONGRESS: DECEMBER, 1865 - JULY, 1866

The first session of the Thirty-ninth Congress convened. December 4, 1865, and immediately became involved in efforts to pass legislation that would give to the Negro certain civil rights. Guided by Radical maneuvers, Congress also became increasingly alienated from President Johnson in the formation of a congressional plan of reconstruction.

A special joint committee was appointed to draft a plan of reconstruction, and throughout the winter and early spring of 1866 it conducted an "investigation" of the South to "prove" its need to be reconstructed. At the same time the committee considered various reconstruction resolutions, bills, and constitutional amendments. The committee was in Radical hands, but the Moderate and Conservative voice reflected enough opinion in Congress to postpone the more extreme measures that came later from the Radical Fortieth Congress.

Simultaneous with committee proceedings was debate in Congress on a civil rights bill that had come from the Committee on the Judiciary in January, 1866. The bill finally passed Congress in April over President Johnson's veto.

The Fourteenth Amendment, which came from the Joint Committee on Reconstruction, was then considered by Congress in May and June. Those opposed to the Amendment attacked the congressional power inherent within it, and some felt the various civil rights measures would give Congress the power to integrate the schools. Those defending the Amendment, however, while usually admitting the change in the balance of power between state and federal government, generally denied that civil rights legislation would affect education.

Charles Sumner, who, in 1870, did introduce a civil rights bill that required school Integration, did not speak in defense of the Fourteenth Amendment in Congress. He said in defense of his later civil rights bill that he believed the Thirteenth Amendment gave Congress all the power it needed to pass legislation designed to give the Negro an equal footing with the white person.

In accord with this belief Sumner introduced several bills and resolutions in December, 1865, that sought to elevate the status of the Negro. On December 4, exactly sixteen years after arguing before the supreme court of Massachusetts the unconstitutionality of separate Negro schools,[1] Sumner proposed by resolution the organization of a school system "for the equal benefit of all without distinction of color or race" as a condition for the admission of the Southern states to representation in Congress. As additional conditions for admission Sumner advocated "impartial" justice and equality before the law and the guarantee of Negro suffrage. On the same day, Sumner proposed two bills--one to enforce the provisions of the Thirteenth Amendment and one to guarantee a republican form of government. Both of these bills were aimed at the realization of equality before the law. In addition to these resolutions and bills, the Senator offered a constitutional amendment that evidently was also related to the guarantee of Negro civil rights.[2]

These proposals by Sumner were not considered by Congress. Neither were similar ones by Thaddeus Stevens, John A. Bingham of Ohio (Rep.), and George S. Boutwell of Massachusetts (Rep.). Stevens desired the Constitution amended so as to make all state and national laws "equally applicable to every citizen."[3] Bingham also wanted to change the Constitution. He suggested that Congress should have the power "to pass all necessary and proper laws to secure to all persons in every State of the Union equal protection in their rights, life, liberty and property."[4] Similarly, Boutwell sought a constitutional amendment to guarantee to the Negro the elective franchise.[5]

All four of these men were prominent in reconstruction debates, and these proposals of December, 1865, were consistent with earlier and later stands. In Roberts v. The City of Boston Sumner defended integrated schools as a necessary aspect of the concept of equality before the law. In his defense of the Thirteenth Amendment, after years of activity in the anti-slavery movement, Sumner mentioned "the right to knowledge and the scored right of family."[6] Also, because of Sumner's efforts racial discrimination was legally eliminated in the selection of witnesses in "the courts of the United States."[7] Writing to John Bright on March 13, 1865, Sumner stated: "I insist that the rebel States shall not come back except on the footing of the Declaration of Independence with all persons equal before the law, and government founded on the consent of the governed."[8]

Bingham, too, was an ardent anti-slavery legislator in the 1850's, and words uttered in debate then were restated in reconstruction arguments. On January 13, 1857, in opposition to the President' a defense of the right to trade slaves within both the slave states and the territories, Bingham said: "The Constitution provides ... that no person shall be deprived of life, liberty, or property, without due process of law. It makes no distinction either on account of complexion or birth--it secures these rights to all persons within its exclusive jurisdiction. This is equality."[9] Then on February 11, 1859, Bingham defended Negro citizenship. The Ohio representative spoke in opposition to the constitution proposed by Oregon for statehood because that document forbade Negroes or mulattoes to enter into the state, to hold property within the state, or to bring suit in Oregon courts. Negroes, maintained Bingham, were United States citizens because of their birth in this country. They were, therefore, entitled to all privileges and immunities guaranteed to United States citizens by Article Four, section two, of the Constitution. This included the "rights of life and liberty and property and ... due protection in the enjoyment thereof by law.'[10] "Natural rights" were to be distinguished from "political rights," continued Bingham. The latter, such as the elective franchise, belonged to "citizens" and could be regulated by the states, so that some citizens would vote and others would not. The former, however, belonged inherently to all "citizens" and to all "persons"--"for example, as expressed in the Fifth Amendment." "The equality of all to the right to live; to the right to know; to argue and to utter, according to conscience; to work and enjoy the product of their toil, is the rook on which that Constitution rests-- its sure foundation and. defense.'[11]

These sentiments were repeated by Bingham in correspondence with Joshua Reed Giddings between 1861 and 1862. "... the slave should be made free because freedom is his right," wrote Bingham on December 19, 1861, and on April 11, 1862: "Sir, our Constitution, the new Magna Charta..., rejects in its bill of rights the restrictive word 'freeman,' and adopts in its stead the more comprehensive words 'no person'; thus giving its protection to all, whether born free or bond. The provision of our Constitution is, 'no person shall be deprived of life, liberty, or property without due process of law.' This clear recognition of the rights of all was a new gospel to mankind... [12]

Both George S. Boutwell and Thaddeus Stevens were particularly interested in securing Negro suffrage--in contrast to Bingham, who felt this to be a matter of state concern. Little was said by either Boutwell or Stevens regarding the guarantee of rights other than suffrage. Stevens did not elaborate upon the scope of the constitutional amendment that he proposed in December, 1865. Its wording, however, suggests that he considered it broader in scope than the granting of just Negro suffrage. Boutwell argued at Weymouth, Massachusetts, July 4, 1865, for the necessity of giving the ballot to the Negro. It would, he said, secure liberties won by the Negro through emancipation--their right to the "integrity of their family," the writ of habeas corpus, the education of their children, and the acceptance of their testimony in court.[13]

Sumner, Bingham, Stevens, and Boutwell were not the only ones participating in this initial civil rights agitation. Sumner's Massachusetts colleague, Henry Wilson, was also active. Consistent with his anti-slavery stand, Wilson introduced a civil rights bill December 13, 1865, that was aimed at the guarantee of "civil rights and immunities" within the rebellious states. Such legislation was necessary, explained the Senator, because southern laws were re-enslaving the Negro.[14] In defense of his bill a week later Wilson stated: "...we must see to it that the man made free by the Constitution of the United States, sanctioned by the voice of the American people, is a freeman indeed; that he can go where he pleases, work when and for whom he pleases; that he can sue and be sued; that he can lease and buy and sell and own property, real and personal; that he can go into the schools and educate himself and his children; that the rights and guarantees of the good old common law are his, and that he walks the earth, proud and erect in the conscious dignity of a free man who knows that his cabin, however humble, is protected by the just and equal laws of his country."[15]

Sumner supported Wilson's bill as it was,[16] but senators John Sherman, Lyman Trumbull of Illinois (Rep.), and Edgar Cowan of Pennsylvania (Rep.), while endorsing the object of the bill, were hesitant to pass this particular bill. Section two of Article Four of the Constitution had guaranteed the rights pertaining to United States citizenship, noted Sherman, but there had, been no power to enforce this guarantee, he explained. Now section two of the Thirteenth Amendment gave Congress the necessary power, but congress should not exercise this power until it had received official notice of ratification of the Amendment. And, by waiting for its ratification, he added, the bill could apply to all the states and not just to the South. The Ohio Senator also felt the language of the bill ambiguous, which might have the effect of destroying all distinctions made because of color. He did not feel Congress should interfere with state law regulating suffrage. The bill, therefore, should enumerate specific rights, concluded. Sherman. "For instance, we could agree that every man should have the right to sue and be sued in any court of justice... and to testify, an incident, an inevitable incident to freedom, without which liberty would be but a name.... We should secure to these freedmen the right to acquire and hold property, to enjoy the fruit of their own labor, to be protected in their homes and family, the right to be educated, and to go and come at pleasure. These are among the natural rights of free men."[17]

Senator Trumbull also believed Congress should wait until ratification of the Thirteenth Amendment before exercising the power granted to Congress by it. In defense of the purpose of the bill Trumbull mentioned the right to personal freedom, to buy and sell, and to make and enforce contracts.[18]

Edgar Cowan expressed approval of the object of the bill, referring specifically to one's right to appear in court either in suit or as a witness, but he believed an additional constitutional amendment necessary to secure these ends.[19]

Senator Reverdy Johnson of Maryland voiced a general skepticism about the desirability of the bill. He was not certain of its effects upon the police power of the state, which, he felt, belonged with the state.[20]

This Wilson bill died during the Christmas recess and was replaced by a Freedman's Bureau bill and a civil rights bill in January. This initial debate concerning the guarantee of civil rights to Negroes was indicative of a general attitude held principally by the Republican majority during this session of Congress. Some sort of legislation was desired that would protect the Negro in his new freedom, that would afford him a civil equality with white men and thus prevent a discrimination in law because of color. Members of the Democratic minority generally opposed such efforts, though not always. Debate about civil rights was not so much concerned with whether or not there was to be a guarantee of civil equality, but, rather, with questions concerning the scope of this guarantee and whether it was to be the state or federal government that would be the guarantor of it.

Lyman Trumbull introduced the Freedmen's Bureau bill and the civil rights bill from the Committee on the Judiciary January 5, 1866. While Sumner, Wilson, and Sherman referred to Negro education when defending civil rights in December, only one person supporting the January civil rights bill mentioned education in his comments. It was not included in the enumeration of rights in these bills, nor was an attempt made to incorporate it within their guarantee of rights. It is difficult, therefore, to ascertain the concept of the bills' scope by those supporting them with regard to Negro education *per se*. There is little difficulty, however, in determining opinions regarding the question of integration. Prior to 1871 only Sumner indicated a belief that integrated schools were required by the concept of equality before the law.[21]

By section six of the Freedmen's Bureau bill schools were to be established for the freedmen.[22] By section seven certain rights were to be guaranteed the Negro: "... to make and enforce contracts, to sue, be parties, and give evidence; inherit, purchase, lease, sell, hold, and convey real and personal property, and to have full and, equal benefit of all laws and proceedings for the security of person and estate."[23] Section one of the civil rights bill, in addition to defining citizenship, and after stating that "there shall be no discrimination in civil rights or immunities" because of race, color, or previous condition of servitude, guaranteed in identical language the rights enumerated in the Freedmen's Bureau bill.[24]

Senator Trumbull, as chairman of the Committee on the Judiciary, reported both these bills. He believed that all legislation devised in the interests of slavery fell with the destruction of that institution. "Those laws that prevented the colored man going from home, that did not allow him to buy or to sell, or to make contracts; that did not allow him to own property; that did not allow him to enforce rights; that did not allow him to be educated, were all badges of servitude made in the interest of slavery and as a part of slavery."[25] By this statement it would appear that the Illinois Senator may have thought education a right inherent in freedom. Neither he nor anyone else, however, made any effort to incorporate reference to education into the civil rights bill when the Freedmen's Bureau bill failed to become law and when the scope of the civil rights bill was possibly reduced by the removal of the declaration that "there shall be no discrimination in civil rights or immunities" because of race, color, or previous condition of servitude.[26] In 1871, in opposition to the Radical interpretation of the Fourteenth Amendment during debate on an enforcement bill, Trumbull said of the 1866 civil rights bill: "... it declared that the rights of colored people should be the earns as those conceded to the white people in certain respects, which were named in the act." [27] In 1872, again in opposition to a Radical reconstruction measure--a civil rights bill requiring Integrated schools--Trumbull denied that education was a "civil right." It was, he maintained, a "privilege," and, further, Integration involved "social equality."[28] While the Senator's thought may have become more "conservative" between 1866 and 1872, it probably did not, so that this later expression was characteristic of his earlier beliefs. He was not associated with the Radical stand taken by Wilson and Sumner in the December, 1865, civil rights debate, and in 1866, while discussing a bill to admit several Southern states to representation in Congress, Trumbull also maintained that civil rights did not include "social rights, or rights in sohool."[29] His thought, then, appears to have remained at a "moderated level throughout this period.

There was little reference to education in debate on the Freedmen's Bureau bill. Senator Reverdy Johnson felt Congress had no power to establish schools anywhere except in the territories.[30] Ignatius Donnelly of Minnesota (Rep.) and Thaddeus Stevens, on the other hand, unsuccessfully worked together in the House to enlarge the powers of the Bureau commissioners to include provision for the education of the refugees and freedmen.[31] Donnelly explained that universal education was necessary if there were universal suffrage, and he offered an amendment secure that end. Then without explanation of his action, Stevens incorporated Donnelly's amendment into a substitute that he offered for the entire bill. Only a few explanatory remarks were made by Stevens about this substitute bill, and it was subsequently defeated.[32] Only one other defense of education was made in debate on the Freedmen's Bureau bill. Josiah B. Grinnell of Iowa (Rep.) called attention to the fact, with particular reference to Kentucky, that without the Bureau the refugees would receive no education.[33] Typical of those that opposed this reconstruction legislation was the stand of John L. Dawson of Pennsylvania (Dem.). He attacked the bill, as a device used by Radicals to bring about a "social equality" between white and black that would include integrated sohools.[34]

Like Dawson, Senator Edgar Cowan feared a required school integration, and he attacked the civil rights bill for this reason. Michael C. Kerr of Indiana (Dem.) also believed the civil rights bill would require integrated schools, and Columbus Delano of Ohio

(Rep.) felt the bill would require states to educate the Negro if they did not already do ao.[35]

Anthony Thornton of Illinois (Dem.) and Senator Garrett Davis of Kentucky also believed the bill would affect areas other than those specifically named, although neither of these men mentioned education.[36] As with all these opponents of the bill, Reverdy Johnson believed the bill struck at "all the reserved rights of the States." If it became law, he felt, it would enable Congress to repeal all state discriminatory legislation. He expressed particular concern for Maryland laws prohibiting intermarriage.[37]

In this civil rights legislation of the first session of the Thirty-ninth Congress the opposition tended to speak of consequences not mentioned and often denied by those defending it. There were cries by the opposition about the invasion of state rights. There was also a broad interpretation of the scope of this legislation by the opposition, with occasional references to education. Those that defended civil rights legislation, on the other hand, while admitting a change in the power structure between state and federal authority, considered the scope of the legislation not so broad as those opposed to it. The defense stated that efforts to protect the Negro in his civil rights were aimed at giving federal protection to only the "fundamental rights" of citizenship and were in no other way to encroach upon state power to legislate in this field. Most of those defending civil rights legislation at this time either felt it would not affect Negro education or did not consider the possibility of their being related.

As chairman of House Committee on the Judiciary, James F. Wilson of Iowa (Rep.) introduced the civil rights bill by saying: Does "equality of citizens mean that in all things civil, social, political, all citizens, without distinction of race or color, shall be equal? By no means" can the term be so construed. It was not a civil right, explained Wilson, for all men to sit upon juries or for their children to attend the same schools. "Civil rights" included only "the absolute rights of individuals" as embraced in Article Four, section two, of the Constitution and defined in Corfield. v. Coryell.[38] This bill would, in fact, not be necessary, said Wilson, if all the states guaranteed these rights to citizens. The bill was only "remedial and protective."[39] Also in this line of argument were Russell Thayer of Pennsylvania (Rep.), William Windom of Minnesota (Rep.), and Samuel Shellabarger (Rep.) and William Lawrence (Rep.) of Ohio, who defended the bill by stating that it guaranteed only those rights specifically enumerated in the bill itself.[40]

Senators Jacob M. Howard of Michigan (Rep.), Trumbull, and. Thomas A. Hendricks of Indiana (Dem.) similarly defined, the scope of the bill.[41]

Between those that categorically either attacked or supported the civil rights bill were those whose stand included both criticism and approval. Henry J. Raymond of New York and John A. Hingham were men of this type of thought. Raymond criticized the punitive section of the bill, which declared that anyone violating the guarantee of civil rights would be subject to fine or imprisonment. He felt this would unjustly punish a judge for upholding in court a law of his state that discriminated in civil rights. The New York representative then offered a substitute for the bill: "That all persons born, or hereafter to be born, within the limits and under the jurisdiction of the United States, shall be deemed and considered, and are hereby declared to be citizens of the United States, and entitled to all rights and privileges as such," In defense of this substitute, which was never considered by the House, Raymond declared his belief that the Negro had the right to "free passage from one State to another," to a home, to defend himself and family, to bear arms, to testify in the federal courts, and to rail those rights" that tended "to elevate and educate him for still higher reaches in the process of elevation."[42]

It is important to know the mind of Bingham in this reconstruction debate, since it was he that framed section one of the

Fourteenth Amendment in committee. His plea for federal guarantee of civil rights is consistent with his ardent anti-slavery stand
prior to the war. Ideas expressed in 1866, in fact, are identical to
those uttered in the 1850s and then again in 1871 when defending
an enforcement bill.

It is difficult, however, to ascertain his concept of the scope of
the civil rights that needed federal protection.

Bingham approved the definition of citizenship within the civil
rights bill. It was, he maintained, simply declaratory of existing
law, that any person born within the jurisdiction of the United
States of parents owing no foreign allegiance was a citizen of the
country, regardless of that person's color.[43]

Bingham disapproved, however, of the fact that the bill guaranteed civil rights only to citizens. By the Constitution all "persons
were guaranteed life, liberty, and property. This bill, therefore,
excluded the "stranger" and "alien" from the proposed federal protection. "The great men who made that instrument [the
Constitution]," explained Bingham, "when they undertook to
make provision, by limitations upon the power of this government,
for the security of the universal rights of man, abolished the nar-
row and limited phrase of the old Magna Charta of five hundred
years ago, which gave the protection of the laws only to 'free men'
and inserted in its stead the more comprehensive words, 'no person'; thereby obeying that higher law given by a voice out of heav-
en: 'Ye shall have the same law for the stranger as for one of your
own country.' Thus, in respect to life and liberty and property, the
people by their Constitution declared the equality of all men, and
by express limitation forbade the Government of the United States
from making any discrimination."[44]

While the Ohio representative wished to expand the guarantee to include all people he felt the scope of that protection in the
civil rights bill too broad. "Civil rights" included "political rights,"
he argued, and therefore this bill would allow Congress to strike

down discrimination "in any of the civil rights of the citizen." Specifically, he noted, with reference to his own state, states would have to relinquish jurisdiction over regulation of the elective franchise and the right to hold office.[45] Bingham then proposed to strike from the bill the general guarantee of civil rights: "... without distinction of color,[46] and there shall be no discrimination in civil rights or immunities among citizens of the United states in any State or Territory of the United States on account of race, color, or previous condition of slavery." His proposal was recommended by the Committee on the Judiciary four days later and then approved by vote of the House.[47]

There was one other objection to the bill made by Bingham, and in this objection lay the genesis of section one of the Fourteenth Amendment. Bingham felt this proposed federal protection of civil rights should be secured through constitutional amendment, rather than by congressional enactment. As it was, he observed, "the enforcement of the bill of rights, touching the life, liberty, and property of every citizen of the Republic within every organized State of the Union, is of the reserved powers of the States...." The restriction of state power, he continued, was in language expressing direct prohibition, as-, no state shall enter into treaty with other powers. The guarantee of civil rights unfortunately had not been fulfilled by voluntary state action, even though state officers had sworn to uphold the Constitution upon taking office. Therefore, the Constitution needed to be amended so as directly to prohibit failure by the state to guarantee civil rights granted in the Bill of Rights. Bingham then drew the attention of the House to an amendment to the Constitution that he had proposed in February of that year, which, though worded differently than the first section of the Fourteenth Amendment, was written with the same object in mind, as section one of the Amendment, By that February amendment, he said, he sought to "arm Congress with the power to compel obedience to the oath administered to state officials ... and to punish all violations by State officers of the bill of rights, leaving state officials with the responsibility of protecting life, liberty, and. property. Standing upon this position, I may borrow the words of the most distinguished man who was ever sent hither from the Old World to make a personal observation of the workings of our institutions, as truly descriptive of the American system: 'centralized government, decentralized administration.' That, sir, coupled with your declared purpose of equal justice, is the secret of your strength and power."[48] To guarantee to all people' their civil rights through both the protection by state government and the power of the federal government -- this was the object of Bingham's effort that culminated in section one of the Fourteenth Amendment.

The amendment to the Constitution of which he spoke in debate on the civil rights bill read: The Congress shall have power to make all laws which shall be necessary and proper to secure to the citizens in the several States, and to all persons in the several States equal protection in the rights of life, liberty, and property." This had been preceded by the amendment offered in December, 1865. In the wording just quoted the amendment was discussed in the Joint Committee of Fifteen,[50] of which he was a member, and introduced by him from committee February 26.[51] In introductory remarks Bingham noted that the amendment was worded in language from the Constitution--Article Four, section two, and a portion of the Fifth Amendment. The only change sought was the grant of power to congress. This change was necessary, he explained, because the states had disregarded the fact that the Constitution was declared to be the supreme law of the land and that their state officers had sworn to uphold that Constitution. If that grant of power had been included in the original Constitution the rebellion "would have been an impossibility."[52]

Why was not this power conferred upon Congress originally? asked Bingham. The answer, he explained, was twofold. First, the framers felt the guarantees of the Constitution sufficient: The Constitution was declared to be the supreme law of the land, state officials were required to swear to uphold that document, and judges in each state were bound by the Constitution. It was felt that with these constitutional requirements states would protect the person from a federal violation of the guarantee of civil rights. Federal power to enforce the Bill of Rights against a violation of it by state government would also have been included, Said Bingham, had it not been for the fact that its insertion would have been "utterly incompatible with the existence of slavery in any State, for although slaves might not have been admitted to be citizens they must have been admitted to be persons." [53]

Because that grant of congressional power was not included, states had been able to avoid the responsibility of enforcing the demands of the Constitution regarding the guarantee of civil rights. Bingham cited two cases involving judicial sanction of this practice. In Barron v. The Mayor and. City Council of Baltimore (7 Peters, 247) Chief Justice Marshall concluded that the Fifth Amendment restrained only the power of the federal government and was not applicable to the states. And in the case of The Lessee of Livingston v. Moore *et. al.* (7 Peters, 551) the Court reiterated this interpretation, with reference to the entire Bill of Rights. [54]

Regardless of this interpretation, however, Bingham felt the amendments constituting the Bill of Rights were to be enforced by the states. To substantiate this belief Bingham quoted Webster: Through the Articles of Confederation the states entered into certain agreements that were to be kept by each state; through the Constitution "the people" spoke to the states in language "'of injunction and, prohibition'" that was to depend on "'individual duty and individual obligation....[the Constitution] lays its hand on individual duty and individual conscience. It incapacitates any man to sit in the Legislature of a State who shall not first have taken his solemn oath to support the Constitution of the United States.

From the obligation of this no State power can discharge him'--(3 <u>Webster's Works</u>, 471)."[55] Bingham could then conclude, in answer to charges that he was invading state rights, that his amendment to the Constitution took from no state any right that belonged to it.[56]

Consideration of this February amendment was postponed until the second Tuesday of April. It was never reconsidered, however, and the Fourteenth Amendment then replaced. it.[57] In his defense of section one of the Fourteenth Amendment Bingham briefly reiterated what he had stated at length in defense of the February proposal: It is the power in the people, the whole people of the United States by express authority of the Constitution to do that by congressional enactment which hitherto they have not had the power to do and never even attempted to do; that is, to protect by national law the privileges and immunities of all the citizens of the Republic and the inborn rights of every person within its jurisdiction whenever the same shall be abridged or denied by the unconstitutional acts of any State... this amendment takes from no State any right that ever pertained to it. No State ever had the right, under the forms of law or otherwise, to deny to any freeman the equal protection of the laws or to abridge the privileges and immunities of any citizen of the Republic, although many of them assumed and exercised the power, and that without remedy.[58]

It was contended in 1871, in debate on a bill to enforce the Fourteenth Amendment, that Bingham withdrew his February amendment because of opposition to it and then advocated adoption of the Fourteenth Amendment as a more moderate measure. Bingham claimed in 1871, however, that the Amendment was more "comprehensive" than his earlier proposal.

He explained that in 1866, upon re-examining the decision in Barron v. The Mayor and City Council of Baltimore, he particularly noticed these words: "Had the framers of these amendments [the first eight] intended them to be limitations on the powers of the State governments they would have imitated the framers of the original Constitution and have expressed that intention." In order to obviate this difficulty Bingham reworded his February amendment to conform with such restraints of state power as, no state shall pass bills of attainder. "Is it not better to prevent a great transgression in advance," asked Bingham, "than to engage in the terrible work of imprisonment and confiscation and execution after the crime has been done? Our fathers in the beginning set us the example of legislating in advance." He then changed the form of the earlier amendment, adding to it the equal protection of the laws clause, which in 1871 he explained in language identical to that used in 1866 in defense of both amendments: "It means that no State shall deny to any person within its jurisdiction the equal protection of the Constitution of the United States, as that Constitution is the supreme law of the land, and, of course, that no State should deny to any such person any of the rights which it guarantees to all men, nor should any State deny to any such person any right secured to him either by the laws and treaties of the United States or of such State."[59]

Both the February amendment and section one of the Fourteenth Amendment had the same object for Bingham--to secure to all citizens of the United States the rights guaranteed to them in the Constitution and to secure to all persons, whether or not citizens their natural rights as embodied in the Constitution through the Bill of Rights. And it is evident by Bingham's defense of both measures in 1866 that he did not vary in his concept of the federal government's acting as the guarantor of these rights in face of state violation of them. Whether either amendment was actually a more powerful proposal than the other in 1866 is a moot question, and the power of either would depend, of course, upon interpretation of it after that date.

The sentiments expressed by Bingham in 1866 were a part of a consistent line of thought to which he held over a long period of years. He declared January 13, 1857, that, under the Constitution as it then stood, "all persons" were to be secure in life, liberty, and property and that no distinctions were to be made because of color or birth.[60] In 1859 Bingham expressed the opinion that all persons born within the jurisdiction of the United States were citizens of the United States and therefore entitled to all privileges and immunities due citizens under section two of Article Four of the Constitution. No state had the right, he observed, to "impair" any of the "natural or inherent rights that belong to all people--for example, as [expressed] in the Fifth Amendment." The "charm" of the Constitution, he claimed, lay "in the great democratic idea which it embodies that all men, before the law, are equal in respect of those rights of person which God gives and no man or State may rightfully take away, except as a forfeiture for orime.[61] In writing to Joshua Reed Giddings April 11, 1862, Bingham spoke of the Constitution as a "new Magna Charta that embraced all people, and not just those free." 'No person shall be deprived of life, liberty, or property without due process of law.' This clear recognition of the rights of all was a new gospel to mankind..."[62]

Bingham expressed these ideas in nearly identical language in 1871, when he defended the bill related to the enforcement of the guarantee of rights within the Fourteenth Amendment.[63] He referred again to the triple guarantee within the Constitution for the securement of civil rights--the oath required to be taken by state officials, the declaration that the Constitution was the supreme law of the land, and the statement that judges were to be bound by the terms of the Constitution. Bingham then quoted once again the words of Webster, that it was upon "individual duty and obligation" that the administration of the Constitution rested. "The states never had the right, though they had the power, to inflict wrongs upon free citizens by a denial of the full protection of the laws," said Bingham. The Fourteenth Amendment supplied a "remedy" for this defect, so that "the nation" could by law provide against "all such abuses and denials of right..."[64] In concluding remarks upon this subject Bingham asked the House "not to forget the imperishable words" of the Declaration, "All men are created equal and endowed by their Creator with the rights of life and liberty." He also asked the House "not to forget those other words of the Declaration that 'to protect these rights (not to confer them) governments are instituted among men'."[65]

The difficulty concerning Bingham's thought is to determine his concept of the scope of the rights he felt Congress should protect. He did not feel the federal government should guarantee what he termed "political rights"--the right to vote and the right to hold office. In 1866 he spoke of privileges and immunities granted citizens under Article Four, section two, and of the right to life, liberty, and property secured to all people by the Fifth Amendment, but he did not enumerate specific rights at this time. He also referred generally to the entire Bill of Rights.

On January 30, 1871, Bingham submitted a majority report from the Committee on the Judiciary that refused to recognize an interpretation of the privileges and immunities clause made by Victoria C. Woodhull in a petition to Congress to include woman suffrage. That clause, stated the report, guaranteed only those rights secured by Article Four, section two, as interpreted in Corfield v. Coryell.[66] In debate on the enforcement bill of that year, however, Bingham expressed the opinion that the privileges and immunities clause was not the same as Article Four, section two. The former declared that a citizen of one state traveling in another state was to be secured rights equal to those conferred upon citizens of the state in which he happened to be. The privileges and immunities clause, on the other hand, granted rights pertaining to United States citizenship, "which are defined in the first eight articles of amendment."[67] Perhaps this shifting can be explained, as a habit of changing emphasis as the new emphasis served to support his opinion on any given subject. Thus he would tend to interpret the Constitution narrowly when either opposed or indifferent to a measure, such as woman suffrage,[68] and would tend to interpret it more broadly when advocating a measure that he favored, such as the federal guarantee of "natural rights."

Even, however, if this explanation makes a contradiction in positions understandable, the question still remains: What was Bingham's understanding of section two of Article Four and of the Bill of Rights, particularly the Fifth Amendment, for in 1866 he referred to these various parts of the Constitution in discussing the two amendments? Did his idea of civil, rights include education, and if it did, was it concerned, with the segregation issue? There were the privileges and immunities enumerated in Corfield v. Coryell: life, liberty, property, pursuit of happiness and safety, movement between states, initiation of proceedings in court, and exemption from taxes higher than paid by others in the same state. In 1859 Bingham stated as "natural rights of citizens and persons the right "to live; the right to know; to argue and to utter, according to conscience; [and] to work and enjoy the product of their toil."[69] In 1866 he referred only generally to the Bill of Rights, with particular stress upon the Fifth Amendment. In 1867, in debate upon a reconstruction bill, Bingham referred to the Negro right to enjoy the reward of his work and the right peaceably to assemble and petition the government for a redress of grievances.[70] In 1871 the Ohio representative mentioned specific rights from the Bill of Rights: to be secure against unreasonable searches and seizures and from the quartering of soldiers in one's home in time of peace without the owner's consent; to be tried by jury, to be informed of the nature of the crime charged against the accused, and to be heard in defense; to receive just compensation for the taking of private property; to have free speech and a free press, and to be able peaceably to assemble for a redress of grievances. He also read to the House the content of each of the first eight amendments to the Constitution.[71]

Only in 1859 did Bingham refer to education as a right, whether this idea carried through into later civil rights legislation is uncertain. It is not unreasonable to assume that it did. His lack of reference to education, however, and his lack of participation in debate on bills related to education certainly indicate either little or no interest in the subject. And there is no mention by Bingham at any time of the segregation issue. Segregation did not actually become a concern of the House until 1874, after Bingham had left both the House and the country as foreign minister to Japan (1873-1885).[72]

While knowledge of the mind of Bingham is highly significant because of his role in framing section one of the Fourteenth Amendment, so, too, is an understanding of the interpretation placed upon the Amendment by other members of Congress, particularly those of the Joint Committee of Fifteen. What did they think of Bingham's February amendment and section one of the Fourteenth Amendment?

Opposition to constitutional amendment as the means by which to guarantee Negro civil equality was at first greater than opposition to the civil rights bill and included more of the Republican majority. The change in the balance of power between state and federal government in the realm of civil rights became more obvious. There was never much opposition to a guarantee of Negro civil equality per ; most congressmen were either eager or willing to prevent a discrimination in law because of color. The argument mainly involved two other questions, namely, was it legitimate for the federal government to act as a guarantor of this civil equality, and what was the scope of this guarantee? As the Republican majority became less "moderate" the former question became less an issue and debate centered mainly in the latter problem.

The voiced opinion about the February amendment was mainly negative. Frederick E. Woodbridge of Vermont (Rep.) was of a minority when he advocated adoption of the amendment. It 'merely gives the power to Congress to enact those laws which will give to a citizen of the United States the natural rights which necessarily pertain to citizenship," he said.[73] It was this "giving" of power to Congress, however, that caused several congressmen to oppose Bingham's efforts. Robert S. Hale of New York (Rep.) charged the amendment with an effect 'more radical...than ever before proposed in any legislative or constitutional assembly.' Thomas T. Davis of New York (Unionist) declared the amendment would invade state power that could not be taken from the states "without a radical and fatal change in their relations to Congress." In the Senate, William I. Stewart of Nevada (Rep.) paused in debate upon reconstruction to condemn Bingham's amendment as a proposition that 'would work an entire change in our form of government.' The first clause was not objectionable, said. Stewart, because it was already within the Constitution as Article Four, section two. By the last clause, however, Congress would have to assume full responsibility for state legislative duties, since "the great body of the laws of the several States as in fact of any government relate to the protection of life, liberty, and property.[74]

Giles W. Hotchkiss of New York (Rep.) feared the amendment would require uniform laws throughout the United States, When Bingham assured him it would not, he stated that the amendment, then, was not so strong as the Constitution, since it already secured equal rights to a certain extent. If Bingham's aim were to prevent discrimination in rights among classes, asked Hotchkiss, why did he not say so directly? Roscoe Conkling of New York, who was a member of the Committee of Fifteen, also expressed dislike of the amendment. His comment was brief and implied that he felt the amendment too radical. Directing his statement to Hotchkiss, he expressed doubt that there could be objection to the amendment because it did not go far enough.[75]

Andrew J. Rogers was more particular in his criticism than the others. He felt the amendment would enable Congress to legislate in the realm of education and, in fact, to require integrated schools "upon the principle that all the people in the several states shall have equal protection in all the rights of life, liberty, and property, and all the privileges and immunities of citizens in the several States."[76]

As previously mentioned, debate on the February amendment terminated February 28, and consideration of the Fourteenth Amendment replaced it. Section one of the Amendment, while framed in its present language by Bingham, evolved out of the deliberations of the Joint Committee of Fifteen along with the other sections of the Amendment. This Committee was organized in December, 1865, for the purpose of examining all reconstruction proposals and constructing a congressional plan of reconstruction. The Republican members from the Senate were William Pitt Fessenden of Maine, James W. Grimes of Iowa, Ira Harris of New York, Jacob N. Howard of Michigan, and George H. Williams of Oregon. The Republican members from the House were John A. Bingham of Ohio, Henry T. Blow of Missouri, George S. Boutwell of Massachusetts, Roscoe Conkling of New York, Justin S. Morrill of Vermont, Thaddeus Stevens of Pennsylvania, and Elihi B. Washburn of Illinois. The only Democratic senator was Reverdy Johnson of Maryland, and. the Democratic representatives were Henry A. Grider of Kentucky and Andrew J. Rogers of New Jersey.

Bingham, Boutwell, Howard, Stevens, and Williams were the most active members in committee. Bingham, Boutwell, Howard, Johnson, and. Stevens were the members of the Committee that was most active in Congress. Fessenden, who wrote the lengthy majority report of the Committee, was absent from it because of illness between April 21 and 25, when there was considerable discussion related to the Fourteenth Amendment.

Stevens, Howard, and Boutwell were Radicals, Washburn, Morrill, and Conkling seem also to be Radicals, but it is difficult to say when judged by civil rights debate, for none were especially active in it. Fessenden was at times Radical but shifted ground between Radical and Moderate forces. Grimes, who admired and. followed Fessenden, seems primarily to have been a Moderate. Grimes was neither active in committee nor in civil rights debate in Congress. Bingham and Williams were Moderates, as Blow and Harris seem to be. The latter two did not participate in civil rights debate, either. Johnson, Grider and Rogers were Conservatives.

While the Committee considered proposals for a congressional plan of reconstruction, sub-committees were organized for the purpose of "investigating" the condition of the South. Several of the questions asked of witnesses in this investigation were related to education: How does the Negro feel about education? What do the whites think of education for the Negro? Would the whites be willing to be taxed to support Negro education? Are there any colored schools? Are the teachers white or black? Are the teachers treated with respect by the community? What is the ability of the Negro to learn? Boutwell, Howard, and Williams were the principal interrogators. other questions asked about the Negro were related to his martial rights and property rights, to the attitude of the white toward Negro suffrage, to the condition of Negro labor, and to the contract rights of the Negro laborer.[78] Since questions about the Negro were generally related to the status of his rights, perhaps these men included education within this category. It is doubtful, however, that either Howard or Williams thought of education in this manner. Boutwell may have.

In defense of the civil rights bill Howard referred only to those rights specifically mentioned in the bill and said nothing of education.[79] When defending the Fourteenth Amendment he stated as its object the guarantee to all that no state would abridge the rights secured by the Bill of Rights and section two of Article Four of the Constitution. In 1869, during debate on the Fifteenth Amendment, Howard again referred to the first section of the Fourteenth Amendment as guaranteeing those rights included within Article Four, section two.[80] In March, 1867, when Sumner proposed as a further reconstruction need the establishment of "public schools for the equal good of all," Howard opposed it. He felt no need to discuss the question since Congress was to examine the Southern state constitutions and would change any provision in them, "either in respect to education or any other subject-matter properly within the scope of State legislation," if not in conformity with the views of Congress.[81] This statement reveals the power assumed by Congress to control reconstruction, but does not necessarily reveal the thought that education was to be considered as a right guaranteed by the Fourteenth Amendment, unless "views of Congress" meant the Fourteenth Amendment. In contrast to this stand is that of Senator Frederick J. Frelinghuysen of New Jersey a few days later. He, too, believed the educational requirement proposed by Sumner not necessary, but his reason was that he thought the Fourteenth Amendment already covered the subject.[82] Howard, instead of voting against Sumner's proposal, as might be expected, voted for it. Frelinghuysen cast a negative vote.[83] Since Howard added nothing to his comments, it is difficult to know why he voted in the affirmative. Perhaps he voted as the issue was drawn by those speaking for it -- there was need for Negro education because the Negro was now a voter.

Another of the principal interrogators of the Committee, Williams, voted against this educational requirement, possibly because he felt it might require integrated schools.[84] If he believed that education were either a right or a need to be given the Negro by Congress one would expect him either to have voted for this amendment or, if objecting to integration, to have offered suggestions to clear up the ambiguity.

At no other time did either Williams or Howard refer to education, and Boutwell referred to it only once between 1865 and 1874. On July 4, 1965, he mentioned education as a right that Negroes needed secured by the ballot.[85] Boutwell, then, like Bingham, may have considered education a civil right throughout the 1860s without indicating a continuity in thought. His primary concern, however, was extension of the ballot to the Negro; education did not occupy his attention until 1874, when he advocated integrated schools as a part of civil rights legislation.

Only two other members of the Committee of Fifteen referred to education--Stevens and Rogers. Stevens felt the Negroes should receive an education through the Freedmen's Bureau; he did not, however, express an opinion about his concept of the nature of education.[86] In July, 1866, Stevens submitted a reconstruction bill to Congress that included as part of section seven: "...no constitution shall be presented to or acted on by Congress which denies to any citizen any right, privileges, or immunities which are granted to any other citizen in the State. All laws shall be impartial, without regard to language, race, or former condition."[87] Stevens, however, never explained what the scope of this requirement might be. In defense of this same bill January 3, 1867, Stevens generally defended equality before the law and ended with this statement: "This doctrine does not mean that a Negro shall sit on the same seat or eat at the same table with a white man. This is a matter of taste which every man must decide for himself. The law has nothing to do with it."[88] The most specific indication of this thought came at his death, when he left money in his will to be used for an orphan home in Lancaster, Pennsylvania, that was to show no preference of color in admission of children. He also provided for his burial in a cemetery where there were no restrictions regarding color or race.[89] Very likely, then, Stevens considered integrated schools a part of his concept of equality before the law; it is difficult, however, to say whether he considered integrated schools a matter of "taste" or a matter of "law." His chief concern, like Boutwell, was the securing of Negro suffrage. Little or no effort was spent on the guarantee of any other specific right.

The only other member of the Committee that spoke of education as a civil right was Andrew J. Rogers, and his comment was in criticism of Republican efforts. If Bingham's February amendment became law, Rogers claimed, Congress could require integrated

It was between January and. April, 1866, that the bulk of testimony was given to the Committee through its sub-committees. During this same time the Fourteenth Amendment evolved out of committee deliberations.[91] The two principal measures that were discussed in the committee in January and February were Bingham's amendment and a proposed constitutional amendment offered by Stevens. This latter amendment declared that whenever the elective franchise was denied because of race or color representation would be proportionately out.

This proposal became the essence of section two of the Fourteenth Amendment, but was debated in Congress as a separate measure in February. It was this amendment that Sumner so vehemently opposed because of the legal recognition of discrimination that it contained. 92

It was in April that the Fourteenth Amendment assumed the form in which it was presented to Congress. On April 16 Senator Stewart came before the Committee to defend a plan of reconstruction advocated by him before the Senate March 16 and April 12. A constitutional amendment prohibited all discrimination because of race or color in "civil rights or the right of suffrage, with the proviso that states might exempt persons then voters from suffrage restrictions that might be imposed.. It also called for the repudiation of the rebel debt. Upon ratification of this amendment a Southern state would be admitted back into Congress with the granting of a "general amnesty."[93]

A rough draft of what is now the Fourteenth Amendment was submitted by Robert Dale Owen through Stevens April 21, and it was this plan of reconstruction that engaged the attention of the Committee. Section one read: "No discrimination shall be made by any state, nor by the United States, as to the civil rights of persons because of race, color, or previous condition of servitude." By section two Negro suffrage was to be granted after July 4, 1876, and by section three representation was to be proportional to the number of voters. Rebel debts were to be repudiated by section four, and a grant of power to Congress to enforce these provisions was the essence of section five. Accompanying this proposed amendment was a plan of reconstruction. Upon ratification of the amendment a Southern state was to be admitted back into Congress, provided, however, that persons participating in the rebellion would be ineligible as members of Congress until July 4, 1876.

On the same day Bingham moved to amend section one of Owen's amendment by adding: "nor shall any state deny to any person within its jurisdiction the equal protection of the laws, nor take private property for public use without just compensation." This motion was defeated, but Bingham than won approval for an additional section to Owen's amendment that is now section one of the Fourteenth Amendment without the citizenship definition.[95] Final committee debate on the Amendment took place April 25 and April 28. On April 25 the Committee agreed to Williams' motion to strike Bingham's section from Owen's amendment and then refused to consider it as a separate amendment. On April 28, however, they agreed to replace section one of Owen's amendment with Bingham's section.[96]

The Fourteenth Amendment and two accompanying reconstruction bills were adopted by the Committee in their final form April 28 and presented to Congress April 30. The two bills provided the terms upon which Southern states could be readmitted to Congress: ratification of the Amendment and payment of whatever amount remained due from the direct tax levied by act August 5, 1861. The bills also barred from eligibility for "any" United States office certain categories of persons, depending upon their war record. These two bills remained unpassed when the first session of the Thirty-ninth Congress adjourned, so that the congressional plan of reconstruction could be interpreted as the political wind might indicate. Reconstruction debate in Congress during May and. June centered upon the Amendment itself, which was finally passed June 13, 1866.

Debate upon the Amendment followed the pattern of that for the civil rights bill and Bingham's February amendment -- those that defended it spoke of limited effects by narrowly defining the scope of the Amendment, while those opposed spoke of the destruction of state rights with federal protection of all personal rights, whether or not specifically enumerated by the Amendment or by those defending it.

Stevens referred generally to the guarantee of the equal protection of the laws, and. Howard felt the Amendment referred only to rights already guaranteed by the Constitution. Stevens, in fact, believed section two to be the most significant.[97] Thomas D. Eliot of Massachusetts (Rep.) spoke approvingly of extending federal power to insure anyone against deprivation of life, liberty, and property or the denial of the equal protection of the laws.[98] John F. Farnsworth of Illinois (Rep.) felt that the terms of the Amendment were already embodied in the Constitution, except the equal protection of the laws clause. "A reaffirmation of a good principle," however, "will do no harm," he explained. Similarly, Senator John B. Henderson of Missouri (Dem.) commented briefly upon the guarantees of section one: "...they merely secure the rights that attach to citizenship in all free Governments. The Amendment also received the support of Henry J. Raymond. He explained that he had opposed the civil rights bill because he felt it unconstitutional. Believing, however, in its object, he would now support section one of the Amendment.[100]

Senator Reverdy Johnson opposed the Amendment. He unsuccessfully moved to strike from it the privileges and immunities clause because, as he explained, he was uncertain of its effect.[101] Also among the opposition were Andrew Rogers and Samuel J.

Randall of Pennsylvania (Dem.). Rogers felt the Amendment would authorize federal regulation of all the rights of citizens of the state, and Randall feared federal regulation of suffrage would be the next step in the Radical attempt to make Negro and white equal[102] Neither of these men referred specifically to education, although Rogers had spoken of it previously in remarks upon Bingham's February amendment.

Of particular significance are the comments of Senator Timothy O. Howe of Wisconsin (Rep.). He was the only one in defense of the Amendment who expressed the belief that it would affect education. After enumerating such rights as holding property, collecting earned wages, and appearing in court as either suitor or witness, Howe stated: ...but, sir, these are not the only rights that can be denied; these are not the only particulars in which unequal laws can be imposed. I have taken considerable pains to look over the actual legislation which has taken place in these several communities with reference to their several constituencies. I could... interest the Senate for a long time by reading from that legislation, but I shall not delay the Senate longer than to call its attention to a single instance. The Senator then spoke of a Florida law by which Negroes were not equal before the law. While both white and black were taxed for white education, only Negroes were taxed for the education of their children; there were not, therefore, sufficient funds for Negro education. Also, the School superintendent could revoke the Negro teaching certificate at will.[103]

It is especially significant that Howe felt the Amendment would affect education, for it indicates the existence of Radical thought linking the subject of Negro education with the guarantee of civil equality expressed in section one at the time Congress passed the Amendment. This is definitely a minority position, both at this time and. until 1872, when education and the Fourteenth Amendment became involved in civil rights debate. Howe is the only one defending reconstruction measures in 1866 who felt the two related.

Sumner occupied the singular position of defending the Negro right to be educated with whites, while at the same time offering no do- tense of the Amendment when framed by Congress. As is evidenced by the substitute bill that he offered for the proposed constitutional amendment related to suffrage and representation, he felt the Thirteenth Amendment granted power to Congress to guarantee all civil rights. In later debate Sumner acknowledged the Fourteenth Amendment as a measure that also conferred power upon Congress to legislate in the field of civil rights. In 1872, for example, he referred to the Amendment as "supplementary to the Thirteenth Amendment.[104]

It is difficult to know exactly the opinion of others who defended civil rights measures regarding its effect upon education. In December, 1865, Wilson and Sherman spoke of education as a civil right, but did not repeat this idea during 1866. Boutwell and Bingham had also expressed this idea prior to 1866, but had failed to reaffirm it. Stevens' concept of equal protection of the laws probably included education, although it is hard to say whether he felt this should be required by law. Securing education as a civil right for these men was obviously not of cardinal importance. Bingham was the most concerned about enforcing the Bill of Rights, and Boutwell and Stevens were most concerned about securing Negro suffrage. Wilson and Sherman were not active in defense of the first section of the Fourteenth Amendment, even though both had defended earlier civil rights legislation. They did not indicate any prime object of consideration, as these other men had.

Of these who had indicated in any way that education should be considered a civil right, only Sumner at this time had indicated support of integration. Stevens should probably be classed with Sumner in this respect, even though he never defended integration in debate. The terms of his will indicate that integration was probably within his definition of equal protection of the laws.

There is one other group that felt there was a tie between education and civil rights legislation. Some of the opposition accused their opponents of trying to regulate education through either the civil rights bill or constitutional amendment. Andrew Rogers, Edgar Cowan, and Michael Kerr specifically expressed a fear of integrated schools should civil rights proposals become law.

The majority, then, of those participating in civil rights debate during the first session of the Thirty-ninth Congress never referred to education as a field included within the scope either of the civil rights bill or the Fourteenth Amendment. Either they must have felt these measures would not affect education or they did not consider the possibility of the two being related.

It is obvious however and important to note that while most men in Congress at this time did not feel Negro education was included within the scope of civil rights legislation, they were generally concerned that there be an equality before the law between Negro and white. The Negro need more than just raw emancipation if inequality in law were not to reduce him to a new form of slavery.

FOOTNOTES: CHAPTER I

1. Argument of Charles Sumner Esq. Against the Constitutionality of Separate Colored Schools, in the Case of Sarah C. Hoberts vs. The City of Boston (Boston: B.F. Roberts, 1849).

2. December 4, 1865, <u>Congressional Globe</u>, 39 Cong., 1 sess., I, 2. Charles Sumner, The Works of Charles Sumner (Boston: Lee and Shepard, 1871-83), X, 17, 26. The content of the constitutional amendment is nowhere recorded. On June 20, 1866, Lyman Trumbull, from the Senate Committee on the Judiciary, recommended that this amendment be indefinitely postponed because it was related to amendments already adopted by Congress (June 20, 1866, <u>Congressional Globe</u>, 39 Cong., 1 sess., IV, 3276-3277).

3. December 5, 1865, <u>Congressional Globe</u>, 39 Cong., 1 sess., I, 10.

4. December 6, 1865 <u>Ibid</u>., I, 14. This proposal by Bingham, who framed section one of the Fourteenth Amendment in committee, is the earliest suggestion of the Amendment.

   There is a distinction made in this study between the power conflict and the question of the scope of civil rights legislation. By the farmer is meant: Was it state or federal authority that was considered to assume responsibility for enforcing the terms of a bill or constitutional amendment? By the latter is meant: What particular rights were considered to be guaranteed by any given piece of legislation--regardless of the question of who was to be the guarantor of those rights?

5. December 13, 1865 <u>Ibid</u>., I, 49.

6. April 8, 1864, <u>Congressional Globe</u>, 38 Cong. 1, sess., II, 1479.

7. June 25, 1864, <u>Ibid</u>., IV, 3261.

8. Edward Pierce, <u>Memoir and Letters of Charles Sumner</u> (Boston: Roberts Brothers, 1877, 1894), IV, 229.

9. January 13, 1857, <u>Congressional Globe</u>, 35 Cong., 2 sess., 1, 984.

10. February 11, 1859, <u>Congressional Globe</u>, 35 Cong., 2 sess., 1, 984.

11. February 11, 1859, <u>Ibid.</u>, I, 985.

12. John A. Bingham to Joshua Reed Giddings, Giddings MSS.

13. George S. Boutwell, <u>Reconstruction: Its True Basis</u> (Boston: Wright and Potter, 1865).

14. December 13, 1865, <u>Congressional Globe</u>, 39 Cong., 1 Sess., I, 39-40.

15. December 21, 1865, <u>Ibid.</u>, I, 111.

16. December 20, 1865, <u>Ibid.</u>, I, 91.

17. December 13, 1865, <u>Ibid.</u>, I, 41-42.

18. December 13, 1865, <u>Ibid.</u>, I, 42-43.

19. December 13, 1865, <u>Ibid.</u>, I, 40-41.

20. December 13, 1865, <u>Ibid.</u>, I, 40.

21. Integration became a matter of concern in Congress between 1871 and 1875, when Sumner led unsuccessful efforts to integrate the schools in both the District of Columbia and the nation.

22. January 12, 1866, <u>Ibid.</u>, I, 210.

23. January 19 1866, <u>Ibid.</u>, I, 318.

24. March 2, 166, <u>Ibid.</u>, II, 1151; March 9, 1866, <u>Ibid.</u>, II, 1293.

25. January 19, 1866, <u>Ibid.</u>, I, 322.

26. Infra, 19.

27. April 11, 1871, <u>Congressional Globe</u>, 42 Cong., 1 sess., I, 75. Infra, 68.

28. May 8, 1872, <u>Congressional Globe</u>, 42 Cong., 2 sess., IV, 3189-3190. Infra, 84.

38. Reference was often made to this section of the Constitution and to this case. Article Four, section two states: "The citizens of each State shall be entitled to all privileges and immunities of citizens in the several States." In Corfield v. Coryell Justice Washington enumerated the following "fundamental"

privileges and immunities as guaranteed by this section: life, liberty, property, pursuit of happiness and safety; writ of habeas corpus, institution of proceedings in the courts; exemption from higher taxes than paid by others. This 1823 case involved a New Jersey statute that prohibited a person who was not at the time a resident of the state from taking or gathering clams, oysters, or shells in the waters of the state on board a vessel not owned by someone residing in the state. The Court upheld the New Jersey statute (11 Washington's Circuit Court Reports, 380).

In 1834, in Crandall v. The State of Connecticut (10 Connecticut, 339), William W. Ellsworth and Calvin Goddard argued that Negroes were citizens of the United States and as such entitled to education as one of the "fundamental rights" outlined by Justice Washington. Prudence Crandall conducted a school for Negroes, and the case followed when she did not comply with a law passed to forbid her teaching Negroes. In the Connecticut Superior Court Judge David Daggett upheld the law and denied the validity of the Ellsworth-Goddard argument on appeal, the decision was reversed, but there was no statement regarding the question of the interpretation of Article Four, section two. The decision was reversed because of "'insufficiency of information'." Bernard C. Steiner, "History of Slavery in Connecticut," Johns Hopkins University Studies, ed. Herbert B. Adams (Baltimore: The Johns Hopkins Press, 1893), XI, 5-52• There was no reference to the Ellsworth-Goddard argument in civil rights debate during Reconstruction.

39. March 1, 1866, <u>Congressional Globe</u>, 39 Cong., 1 sess., II, 1117-1118.
40. March 2, 1866, <u>Congressional Globe</u>, 39 Cong., 1 sess., II, 1151-1152, 1159; March 9, 1866, <u>Ibid.</u>, II, 1293-1294; April 7, 1866, <u>Ibid.</u>, II, 1832-1833.

41. January 30, 1866, <u>Ibid.</u>, I, 5011; February 2, 1866, <u>Ibid.</u>, I, 599-600, 601-602.
42. March 8, 1866, <u>Ibid.</u>, II, 1266.
43. March 9, 1866, <u>Ibid.</u>, II, 1291.
44. March 9, 1866, <u>Ibid.</u>, II, 1292.
45. March 9, 1866, <u>Ibid.</u>, II, 1291.
46. This phrase was the concluding statement in the definition of citizenship. Bingham evidently felt it superfluous.
47. March 9, 1866, <u>Ibid.</u>, II, 1296; March 13, 1866, <u>Ibid.</u>, II, 1366. The vote was not recorded.
48. March 9, 1866, Ibid., II, 1291-1292. Undoubtedly Bingham was referring here to de Tocqueville. In volume one of Democracy in America there is a sub-chapter entitled "Political Effects of Decentralized Administration in the United States" in which de Tocqueville discusses "centralized government" and "decentralized administration."
49. While the question regarding the meaning of "person"-- whether Bingham considered it to include corporations-- is not a formal part of this paper, it is very much involved in the material examined and presented here. It is my opinion that Hingham did not mean to include protection of corporations within section one of the Fourteenth Amendment. In addition to the repeated use of "person" as though he meant only the individual personality, there is a bill reported by him from the Committee on the Judiciary that stands in contrast to the interpretation that includes corporation within the definition of "person." In February, 1871, he defended a bill "extending to corporations the privileges and immunities guaranteed by the Constitution to the citizens of the respective States." With reference to insurance companies, Bingham argued that corporation owners were citizens and as such entitled to the guarantee of their privileges and immunities. This bill, a substitute for an original, called for the protection of a corporation from a pen-

alty levied by a state against an action by a corporation that was authorized by national law. The bill also sought to give protection to a corporation in any state equal to that given by the state to its own citizens in matters of trade and. commerce.

The original bill, which is not recorded, had been broader in scope, and Bingham explained that the Committee felt the original was not constitutional. There was no action taken upon the substitute bill after a brief discussion concerning state regulation of insurance companies. (February 16, 1871, Congressional Globe, 41 Cong., 3 sess., II, 1288-1290.)

50. This committee was organized in December, 1865, for the purpose of examining all reconstruction proposals and framing a congressional plan of reconstruction. Infra,3S.
51. February 26, 1866, Congressional Globe, 39 Cong., 1 sess., II, 1033-1034.
52. February 26, 1866, Ibid., II, 1034.
53. February 28, 1866, Ibid., II, 1090.
54. February 28, 1866, Ibid., II, 1089-1090. Barron v. The Mayor and City Council of' Baltimore was the first in a series of decisions that interpreted the Bill of Rights as a restriction only upon federal power. This case involved the taking of private property for public use. The Lessee of Livingston v. Moore *et. al.* was another such case.
55. February 28, 1866, Ibid., II, 1090.
56. February 28, 1866, Ibid., II, 1088-1089.
57. February 28, 1866, Ibid., II, 1095. II
58. May 10, 1866, Ibid., III, 2542.
59. March 31, 181 Congressional Globe, 42 Cong., 1 sess., II, "Appendix," 83-85.
60. January 13, 1857, Congressional Globe, 34 Cong., 3 sess. II, "Appendix," 140.
61. February 11, 1859, Congressional Globe, 35 Cong., 2 sess., I, 981-985.

62. John A. Bingham to Joshua Reed Giddings, April 11, 1862, Giddings MSS.

63. This bill was debated March and April, 1871, and passed April 19. Infra, 69.

64. March 31, 1871, Congressional Globe, 42 Cong., 1 sess., II, "Appendix," 85.

65. Op. cit.

66. Reports of the Committees of the House of Representatives 1870-1871, 41 Cong., 3 sess., doc. no. 22, ser. 1464.

67. March 31, 1871, Congressional Globe, 42 Cong., 1 sess., II "Appendix," 84.

68. It can only be assumed that Bingham, as most men and women at the time, either opposed women suffrage or federal protection of it or were indifferent to the question. No opinions on the subject by Bingham are recorded, which suggests at least that he had no particular concern for the issue.

69. February 11, 1859, Congressional Globe, 35 Cong., 2 sess., I, 985.

70. January 16, 1867, Congressional Globe, 39 Cong., 2 sess., I, 504. Infra, 55. Bingham at this time also referred to the Negro right to participate in the reorganization of the governments of the insurgent States," which stands in contrast to his belief that it was a state right to regulate "political rights."

71. March 31, 1871, Congressional Globe, 42 cong., 1 sess., II, "Appendix," 84, .

72. Letters from Bingham to his daughter, Emma, during this period in Japan contain no reference to the civil rights issue of 1872-1875. Bingham MRS.

73. February 28, 1866, Congressional Globe, 39 Cong., 1 sess., II, 1088.

74. February 27, 1866, Ibid., II, 1063; February 28, 1866, Ibid., II, 1082, 1087.

75. February 28, 1866, <u>Ibid.</u>, II, 1095.

76. February 26, 1866, <u>Ibid.</u>, V,"Appendix," 134.

77. This classification is based upon the activities of these men during the first session of the Thirty-ninth Congress as recorded in the journal of the proceedings of the Committee, in congressional debates, and in biographical materials, particular emphasis was placed upon their opinion regarding Negro suffrage and upon their voting record both in committee and in Congress.

78. The Report of the Joint Committee on Reconstruction at the First Session Thirty-Ninth Congress, 1866.

79. January 30, 1866, <u>Congressional Globe</u>, 39 Cong., 1 sess., I, 504.

80. May 23, 1866, <u>Ibid.</u>, III, 2765-2766; February 8, 1869, <u>Ibid.</u>, II, 1003.

81. March 11, 1867 <u>Congressional Globe</u>, 40 Cong., 1 sess., 56.

82. March 16, 1867, <u>Congressional Globe</u>, 40 Cong., 1 sess., 167.

83. March 16, 1867, <u>Ibid.</u>, 170.

84. March 16, 1867, <u>Ibid.</u> 169. <u>Infra.</u> 58.

85. George S. Boutwell, <u>Reconstruction: Its True Basis</u>.

86. February 5, 1866, <u>Congressional Globe</u>, 39 Cong., 1 sess., I, 655, February 6, 1866, <u>Ibid.</u>, I, 618.

87. July 28, 1866, <u>Ibid.</u>, V, O31304.

88. January 3, 1867, <u>Congressional Globe</u>, 39 Cong., 2 sess., I, 252.

89. Richard Current, <u>Old Thad Stevens</u> (Madison: The University of Wisconsin, 1942), 285, 320. Stevens' will was published in the <u>New York Tribune</u>, August 19, 1868.

90. February 26, 1866, Congressional Globe, 39 Cong., 1 sess., V, Appendix, 134.

91. The record of committee proceedings is in a journal kept by the Committee. Debate, however, was not recorded, so that the journal is a guide only to motions and. votes.

92. February 5-6, 1866, Ibid., I, 673-667 On February 2 Sumner
    had given notice of the following joint resolution, offered as a
    counter measure to the proposed amendment related to suf-
    frage and representation, which he said he would call from
    the table at a future date: "That in all States lately declared to
    be in rebellion there shall be no oligarchy, aristocracy, caste,
    or monopoly invested with peculiar privileges or powers, and
    there shall be no denial of rights, civil or political, on account
    of color or race; but all persona shall be equal before the law,
    whether in the court room or at the ballot-box; and this stat-
    ute, made in pursuance of the Constitution, shall be the su-
    preme law of the land, anything in the constitution or laws of
    any such State to the contrary notwithstanding." (February 2,
    1866, Ibid., I, 592.) On March 9 Sumner moved the adoption
    of an identical resolution, with the exception that it was direct-
    ed to all the states, and not just those of the South. To make it
    more acceptable to the Senate, however, he modified it so that
    it would relate only to the Southern states. This resolution,
    moved as an act of Congress to replace the proposed constitu-
    tional amendment, was defeated 8-39. (March 9, 1866, Ibid.,
    II, 1283-1287.) Then on March 12 Sumner offered a substitute
    constitutional amendment that was the same as the original,
    except there was no reference to color, race, or previous condi-
    tion of servitude, thus eliminating the recognition of discrimi-
    nation that he so much despised. No action was taken upon
    this substitute, and there was also no further debate upon the
    original amendment after this date. (March 12, 1866, Ibid., II,
    1321.)
93. March 16, 1866, Ibid., II, 1437; April 12, 1866, Ibid., II, 1906.
    Benjamin B. Kendrick, The Journal of the Committee of
    Fifteen on Reconstruction (New York: Columbia University,
    1914), 82.

94. Benjamin B. Kendrick, op. cit., 83-84. Owen wrote of his plan in June, 1875, in the <u>Atlantic Monthly</u>. He stated at that time that Stevens and Sumner felt the plan too lenient, Fessenden approved it, and Bingham, Boutwell, Conkling, Howard, and Washburn also approved of it in varying degrees of enthusiasm. The Democrats "held back," he reported. Owen went on to offer his explanation of why the plan was not adopted by the Committee as it had been proposed. His amendment was to have been accepted by the Committee, but they postponed action for a few days so that Fessenden could participate in debate; he was ill with the varioloid. In the meantime, Stevens had explained to Owen, news of the amendment reached the public and there was then pressure from New York, Illinois, and. Indiana to eliminate the section extending suffrage rage to the Negro. The Committee acquiesced in the face of this pressure and the result was the plan reported by the Committee April 30. (Robert Dale Owen, "Practical Results from the Varioloid," <u>Atlantic Monthly</u>, XXXV (1875), 660-670.)

95. Benjamin B. Kendriok, <u>op. cit</u>., 85-87. The definition of citizenship was added in the Senate by Howard May 30 (<u>Congressional Globe</u>, 39 Cong., 1 sess., IV, 2890-2897).

96. Kendrick, <u>op. cit</u>., 98-99, 106-107. In voting for or against Bingham's section on the three days, April 21, 25, 28, no one, except Bingham, voted consistently. Since no debate was recorded, it is difficult to explain this shifting.

97. May 8, 1866, <u>Congressional Globe</u>, 39 Cong., 1 sess., III, 2459; May 23, 1866, <u>Ibid</u>., III, 2765-2766.

98. May 9, 1866, <u>Ibid</u>., III, 2511.

99. May 10, 1866, <u>Ibid</u>., III, 2539; June 8, 1866, <u>Ibid</u>., IV, 3031.

100. May 9, 1866, <u>Ibid</u>., III, 2502-2503• Raymond opposed section three, which called for the disfranchisement of Southern

whites. This provision, of course, was later changed to restrictions upon office-holding by Southerners. Raymond voted for
the Amendment in its amended form.

101. June 8, 1866, <u>Ibid.</u>, IV, 3041.
102. May 10, 1866, <u>Ibid.</u>, III, 2538, 2530.
103. June 5, 1866, <u>Ibid.</u>, V, "Appendix," 219.
104. January 31, 1872, <u>Congressional Globe</u>, 42 Cong., 2 sess., I, 728.

CHAPTER 2

CONGRESS: 1866-1872

Further consideration of the Fourteenth Amendment did not occupy Congress until 1871, when debate upon a bill to enforce the guarantee of rights within the Amendment reined only the question of the extent to which the Amendment conferred power upon Congress to act in a field formerly reserved to the states. There was virtually no comment at this time about the scope of the constitutional guarantee of civil equality--what specific rights were guaranteed.

Between 1866 and 1872 the question of Negro education was of minor importance in reconstruction debate and seems to be related only incidentally to the more important congressional efforts to extend the suffrage to the Negro and to establish Radical state governments in the South. When there was comment about Negro education during these five years it generally, though not always, accompanied remarks about Negro suffrage--the Negro needed to be educated, it was said, now that he was becoming a voter.

There were a few significant comments that indicate a belief at this time that the Fourteenth Amendment would require states to educate the Negro, and in such a way as to prevent any discrimination from being made. These remarks, however, are by no means characteristic of comments about Negro education at this time.

The evidence from congressional debates between 1866 and 1872 regarding either the Fourteenth Amendment or Negro education supports the conclusion that most of those responsible for the passage of the Amendment either believed the Amendment would not affect the realm of education or did not consider the possibility of the two being related in any way. There were congressional efforts after 1866 and prior to 1872 to help with the education of the Negro, and during this same period there were congressional efforts to enforce a guarantee of equality before the law for the Negro. Except for a few notable exceptions, however, these two endeavors remained separate and distinct.

As for school integration, this was not considered by Congress until Sumner introduced a civil rights bill that included provision for such. It was at this time, between 1872 and 1875, that Congress first sought to interpret the meaning of the Amendment with regard to separate Negro schools.

It may be suggested that in 1872 Sumner merely gave expression to a more general congressional belief that schools should be integrated because of the guarantee of civil equality both within the Civil Rights Act of 1866 and the Fourteenth Amendment. If this were so, however, one would expect Congress to have integrated the schools in the District of Columbia. All bills related to Negro education in the District between 1866 and 1870, however, were directed toward the separate schools that had been established for them prior to and after the framing of the Fourteenth Amendment in Congress, and no one questioned this segregation when considering these bills.[1] lt was Sumner himself who introduced legislation to integrate the schools in the District,[2] and this effort, which failed,[3] had been preceded by earlier successful efforts also directed toward the securement of equal rights in the District of Columbia.[4]

It must be concluded, then, that prior to 1872 the general distinction in debate between comments related to Negro education and comments related to the enforcement of the Fourteenth Amendment were characteristic of a distinction between the two subjects within the minds of most congressmen at the time.

As noted, comment upon Negro education between 1866 and 1872 was generally made only with reference to the Negro's need for education because of his enfranchisement, with particular emphasis placed upon the granting of Negro suffrage. This line of thought is evident in debate on the various reconstruction bills that were considered by Congress after 1866.

In 1867 the second session of the Thirty-ninth Congress and the first session of the Fortieth Congress passed several measures designed to reconstruct the South. None of the bills adopted contained provision for Negro education, however.

The first of these bills was the one introduced by Stevens in July, 1866, and discussed by Congress in January, 1867. Section seven of this bill demanded that Southern constitutions provide for equality before the law. This section also stated that a Southern state would lose its right to representation in Congress should this guarantee of equality "ever be altered, repealed, expunged, or in any way abrogated." There was neither elaboration upon the meaning of Stevens' requirement of equality nor a questioning of it. It was the latter provision that drew criticism from the House. Bingham, for example, expressed his desire to grant equal rights, but he was not willing to take from the people their right to alter their constitutional government. Stevens eventually withdrew the section because, as he explained, it had been "somewhat objected to."[5]

James M. Ashley of Ohio (Rep.) offered a substitute for Stevens' bill in which there was the requirement that Southern state constitutions provide for a school system from which no child was to be excluded because of race or color.[6] Ashley withdrew this substitute a few weeks later. No comment was made upon his provision for education; most of the discussion on reconstruction during these weeks was on Stevens' bill.

It was in March, 1867, that debate about Negro education began. On March 7 Sumner introduced a series of resolutions enacting "certain further guarantees required in the reconstruction of the rebel States." These resolutions were similar to those submitted by him in December, 1865, and called for the establishment of provisional governments, the checking of rebel influence, the establishment of common schools 'for the equal good of all,' and the granting of land to freedmen.[7]

Sumner spoke of the Negro's need for education because of his being granted the suffrage.[8] John Sherman felt the resolution on education unnecessary, however, since the South knew it would have to educate its children, white and black. And the federal government had no power, he maintained, to step in to aid the states in this task. Senator Howard also felt there was no necessity for the resolution since Southern constitutions, framed according to the public sentiment of each state, were to be submitted to Congress for examination. If at that time Congress believed any constitution defective it would require a change to make it conform to congressional policies.[9] Timothy O. Howe, on the other hand, defended this resolution as the most important of those proposed by Sumner. Education was necessary to strengthen republican institutions, said the Wisconsin Senator, and it was also necessary for the Southern states to recognize one's "right" to be educated.[10]

Senator Oliver P. Morton of Indiana also supported Sumner's educational resolution. He thought it a legitimate requirement sine education was the complement of suffrage. He also felt it better to inform the states of congressional requirements before conventions convened to frame new constitutions than to wait until: the constitutions were submitted to Congress. Morton had been elected to Congress in the 1866 election and had not, therefore, been a member of the session framing the Fourteenth Amendment. As governor of Indiana, however, Morton had praised Radical efforts and had defended Negro suffrage. In his last gubernatorial message he had also recommended to the Indiana legislature that it change state law excluding the Negro from the public schools. He had added, however, that it would be better to educate Negroes in separate schools so as not to create dissatisfaction and conflict that would impair the usefulness of the schools."[11]

There was no further comment upon Sumner's resolutions, and he eventually withdrew them July 3. On March 16, 1867, he again made an effort in behalf of education. He moved to amend the supplementary reconstruction bill then under consideration to require the Southern states to provide by their constitutions for the establishment of a public school system "open to all, without distinction of race or color.[12] Morton again defended Sumner's proposition, referring to the need for education as a part of republican government. Morton's colleague in the senate and political rival in Indiana, Thomas A. Hendricks, opposed Sumner's amendment. He felt Congress had no power to declare in advance what a state constitution must contain.[13]

James W. Patterson of New Hampshire (Rep.), who had been inactive in debate on the Fourteenth Amendment during its consideration by Congress, questioned the constitutionality of Sumner's March amendment. Would not confiscation of Southern property be necessary to establish a school system similar to that in New England? In reply Sumner said nothing of confiscation, but indicated that a system could be established on the New England pattern. With his fears evidently quieted, Patterson voted for the amendment.[14] Senator George H. Williams also questioned Sumner: Would his amendment require integrated schools? Sumner indicated his desire that they be so, but stated the amendment was "necessarily general in its character" and did not go into detail."

The object of the amendment, said the Senator, was simply to have the Southern states make provision for free schools.[15]

There were two other senators commenting upon Sumner's proposal that had not been members of the first session of the Thirty-ninth Congress -- Cornelius Cole of California (Rep.), who repeated Morton's views in defending the amendment, and Frederick T. Frelinghuysen of New Jersey (Rep.). The comments of Frelinghuysen are significant because they offer the first congressional interpretation of the scope of the first section of the Fourteenth Amendment after the Amendment passed Congress, and the Senator joined Senator Rowe of Wisconsin in expressing the idea that education would be included within the Amendment's demand for equality. Generally the New Jersey Senator felt it was not the way "to do business to require certain things of Southern states and then to add to those requirements after efforts were being made to meet the original demands. Specifically, Frelinghuysen believed the amendment unnecessary since the Fourteenth Amendment required the object of it and since the Amendment had to be ratified by each state before it was given representation in Congress.[16]

Sumner's amendment was defeated, but several months later, in July, he again brought it before the Senate. At this time his proposal was ruled out of order because it was not necessary to execute former reconstruction legislation.[17]

These initial efforts to reconstruct the South were instituted, therefore, without any requirement for education, and Sumner lamented the fact that they had been. [18]

In 1868 another effort was made to include education in reconstruction legislation, but again it was defeated. It was Senator John B. Henderson of Missouri (Dem.) who tried unsuccessfully to incorporate an educational condition into the bill to admit Arkansas. He felt this was necessary because of the extended suffrage.[19]

In debate upon the Arkansas bill there was an interesting discussion between Henderson and Frelinghuysen. Henderson's suggestion to include education within the fundamental conditions of admission had been framed in the following language: "Upon the fundamental condition that said State, in fixing the qualifications of electors therein, shall not be authorized to discriminate against any person on account of race, color, or previous condition; and also upon the further condition that no person on account of race or color shall be excluded from the benefit of education or be deprived of an equal share of the moneys or other funds created or used by public authority to promote education in said State." Henderson moved this as an amendment or substitution for an amendment to the bill proposed by Charles D. Drake of Missouri (Rep.): "...there shall never be in said State any denial or abridgment of the elective franchise, or of any other right to any person by reason or on account of race or color, excepting Indiana not taxed...."[20]

In discussion with Freylinghuysen, who defended Drake's amendment, Henderson objected to "any other right." "I think that includes civil rights," said. Henderson. "I should like to ask the Senator from New Jersey whether, upon the adoption of this amendment of my colleague, in his judgment the State is permitted to provide separate schools for whites and blacks, or whether they must not be educated in the same schools?"

Freylinghuysen replied: I cannot answer that question, for I do not think that either the (fourteenth) constitutional amendment or the proposition of the Senator's colleague touches that question, as to what school they shall be educated in; but I think the amendment as proposed, as well as the constitutional amendment, prevents a discrimination in civil and political rights on account of race or color." Henderson then stated his view:"Mr. President, I can state in a few words my view in offering this amendment. I desire that the negroes shall have an equal right in the school moneys, but that the State may require them to be educated in different schools from the whites. I propose that their rights shall be the same in the public funds, just as we have provided in the District of Columbia."

Henderson's amendment was defeated and Drake's accepted, so that the Arkansas bill was framed in language having direct reference only to the elective franchise.[21] This is the first instance in Congress in which there was a defense of the separate but equal doctrine. It is also the first time that an interpretation was given to the Fourteenth Amendment with regard to the question of segregation.

When a bill to admit North Carolina, Louisiana, Georgia, Alabama, and Florida was before Congress in 1868 Senator Trumbull made certain there would be no ambiguity in its requirements for admission. The terms of this bill had been drawn in language identical to that of the Arkansas bill. Speaking for the Committee on the Judiciary Trumbull recommended striking "or any other right" from the bill. There was no necessity for this phrase, he explained, and there was no reason to give cause for misunderstanding. The citizens of the states were already protected in their "civil rights," and there might be confusion as to the meaning of "any other right"; it might apply to "social rights, or rights in schools, which the Senator from Missouri [Drake] did not intend." The recommendation of Trumbull was accepted by the Senate, and the fundamental conditions were framed in language having no possible relation to education.[22]

In the two years between the consideration of the Fourteenth Amendment in Congress and its ratification in 1868, then, no provision was made for Negro education within reconstruction legislation, and comment on the few efforts to do so generally referred only to the need for the Negro to be educated because of his new status within society. There were, however, a few significant references to the Fourteenth Amendment when discussing Negro education. Frelinghuysen had expressed his belief that Southern states would be required by the Amendment to provide for Negro education. He did not feel, however, that the Amendment was related to the question of integration. Senator Henderson, on the other hand, feared an undefined call for civil equality might require schools to be integrated and expressed for the first time in Congress a belief that separate schools equally supported by school funds would be consistent with efforts to prevent discriminations made because of race or color.

Not until 1870 was there further consideration of bills to admit reconstructed Southern states, and at this time the states were required never to change their constitutional guarantee of a public school education for all children regardless of race or color. By this time the Fifteenth Amendment had been passed by Congress, and this culminating effort to extend the suffrage to the Negro had undoubtedly heightened interest in Negro education to the point where reconstruction bills in 1870 contained education requirements, whereas those of 1867-1868 had not.

Again, comments in defense of Negro education generally referred to the Negro's need to be educated. There was, however, one additional reference to the Fourteenth Amendment in these discussions, and there were also additional expressions of fear that Radical efforts might cause the schools to be integrated.

Senators Howard and. Horton defended these 1870 reconstruction requirements that educational guarantees within Southern constitutions not be altered. They referred to the need for the Negro to be educated and said education was a means by which to safeguard and secure the republican form of government.[23] Trumbull and Bingham briefly referred to the educational provisions of the constitutions and also expressed general approval of them.[24]

Senator Stewart was the only one in 1870 who offered any specific comment about education and. the Fourteenth Amendment. When speaking about the bill to admit Mississippi the Nevada Senator stated that the first section of the Amendment, considered with the civil rights bill and the Fifteenth Amendment, autho-rized the exercise 'of a good deal of controlling power to keep these [southern] people straight. "The States shall make no discrimination in their laws. I believe if the State of Mississippi should pass a law which would deprive the colored man of the same rights and privileges of schools that the white man has, or make any other discrimination which would deny him the equal protection and benefit of the laws, we have direct constitu-tional power to interfere...[25] In 1874, in debate on a civil rights bill that raised the question of school integration, Stewart was among those defending the constitutionality of the bill. He also felt there was constitutional authority to require integration, but he believed it would be better to have the states settle this ques-tion for themselves.[26]

Those who criticized the educational provisions of the new Southern constitutions, both in 1868 and. in 1870, pointed to a Radical demand for integrated schools, just as some of the Democratic opposition had in 1866 when opposing efforts to guarantee to the Negro civil equality with the white person. James Brooks of New York (Dem.), who had been a member of the first Session of the Thirty-ninth Congress, objected to the constitution of Alabama. He believed it required a voter of the state to pledge himself "for all time to negro voting, to fellow negro soldiers, to ne-gro jurymen, to negro and white mongrel school-houses, to mon-grel oars, to mongrel taverns, to a complete mongrel existence from the cradle to the grave.[27] Two others, who had entered Congress in 1867, also opposed requirements for education in Southern consti-tutions. James Beck of Kentucky (Dem.) attacked the constitution of Arkansas because he believed it required schools to be integrat-ed, and Senator Allen. Thurman of Ohio (Dem.) objected to the requirement in the Mississippi constitution for public schools. Be believed neither universal suffrage nor public education was a nec-essary aspect of republican government.[28]

Southern schools under Radical supervision were not integrated, however, except for those in Louisiana. Integration was not the burning issue in Congress at this time, and the Southern states were left to settle this question for themselves. If Congress had expected them to integrate their schools, however, because it was felt segregation would fall short of the Fourteenth Amendment's demand for equality, one would have expected Congress to pass legislation integrating the schools in the District of Columbia. 3eoauee they did not do this, one is left with the impression that congressmen either believed segregation consistent with the concept of equality before the law or did not believe the question of segregation to be included within the scope of the requirements of section one of the Amendment.

Prior to 1872 Congress was primarily concerned with extending the suffrage to the Negro and with efforts to set Southern states up under Radical control. Concern for Negro education seems largely to be incidentally related to these efforts and was not yet encompassed within congressional agitation for the guarantee of civil equality.

Two education bills considered during Reconstruction again prompted the observation that the Negro needed an education because of his new status, while a bill related to the enforcement of the guarantee of rights within the Fourteenth Amendment did not provoke any discussion about Negro education.

In 1867 a bill was passed providing for the establishment of a department of education. In debate upon this bill there was no reference to the Fourteenth Amendment. Samuel W. Moulton of Illinois (Dem.), who had voted for the Amendment in 1866, did refer to the Civil Rights Act, but as though it and education were two distinct subjects related only as complements to strengthen the republic. Because of the war and the Civil Rights Act universal liberty was guaranteed, he explained; now universal education was needed as the other pillar to make strong the American

Republic.[29] Ignatius Donnelly referred to the need to give wise direction to the new power conferred upon the Negro in remarks defending the bill,[30] and Senator Howe also spoke again in defense of both suffrage and education.[31]

Then between 1870 and 1874 there was an unsuccessful attempt to establish a national education fund to be used for the benefit of education in all the states. It was to be derived from the sale of public lands. Again there was no reference to the Fourteenth Amendment, even though the question of the Amendments relation to education had been raised in civil rights debate. George F. Boar of Massachusetts, who introduced, the bill, desired to keep the ignorant Negro from the control of "scheming politicians," and John Coburn of Indiana (Rep.), Hilo Goodrich of New York (Rep.), and Henry L. Dawes of Massachusetts stressed the need for Negro education because of his new freedom. Dawes referred particularly to the Fifteenth Amendment in speaking of the Negro's growing political power and his need for education.[32]

Those opposed to the national Education bill pointed to integrated schools as part of the purpose of the advocates of the bill, just as those opposed to Radical Southern constitutions had in discussing the readmission of Southern states. Michael C. Kerr indicated, this belief, as he had in criticizing the civil rights bill in 1866. John R. Bird of New Jersey (Bern.), John P. Harris of Virginia (Bern.), and Henry D. McHenry of Kentucky (Bern.), all of whom became members of Congress after 1866, also felt integrated schools would be required if the bill became law.[33] John B. Storm of Pennsylvania (Dem.), who was elected to Congress in 1870, opposed this education bill, too, and expressed the belief that Radical interpretation of the Fourteenth Amendment would require integrated schools if under this bill they were not established. Within a year, he claimed, the bill would have to meet the demands of Sumner's pending civil rights bill.[34]

The Democratic opposition continually expressed the fear that Radical efforts to guarantee civil equality and to provide for Negro education might bring about an integration of the schools, and Senator Henderson of Missouri, in an of- fort to avoid, this possibility, first gave expression to the separate but equal doctrine. Senators Howe, Frelinghuysen, and Stewart, however, were the only three supporting Radical efforts before 1872 who expressed the idea that education would be affected by the Amendment's demand for equality. Also, none of these men felt the Amendment necessarily called for integration, although both Howe and Stewart in civil rights debate in the 1870's expressed their belief that a civil rights bill requiring schools to be integrated would be constitutional. Frelinghuysen, on the other hand, in 1868, had said the Amendment did not have anything to say about the question of integration.

In 1871 Congress became involved, in debate about the Fourteenth Amendment for' the first time tine its passage and subsequent ratification. This discussion was generally related to the question of the extent to which the Amendment conferred power upon Congress to act in a field hitherto reserved to the states. There was little comment at this time upon the scope of the Amendment's guarantee of civil equality -- what specific rights were guaranteed by it.

The object of this 1871 bill was the enforcement of the guarantee of rights in the Fourteenth Amendment. This was an effort directed against the activities of the Ku Klux Klan, which had been noted in several resolutions and bills introduced in March, 1671' On March 23 President Grant sent a message to Congress advising it to pass legislation to secure "life, liberty, and property, and the enforcement of law." On March 28 Samuel Shellabarger of Ohio (Rep.) introduced a bill in the House from the select committee organized to consider the President's message. The bill sought to protect the "rights...privileges... [and] immunities" of individuals as guaranteed by the Constitution. Penalties were provided for the violation of these guarantees by any individual or group. In his introductory remarks Shellabarger noted that the Amendment required states not to abridge "the rights of citizenship" and to protect "all persons equally." Shellabarger referred to Corfield v. Coryell for an enumeration of rights that "inhere in citizenship."[35]

Those who had been members of the first session of the Thirty-ninth Congress were divided in their interpretation of the power that the Fourteenth Amendment conferred upon Congress, and while their division was identical to positions taken in 1866, the nature of their argument differed at times. The Conservative opposition denied the existence of a congressional power that they had attacked in 1866 as inherent within Radical efforts, and Radical arguments in 1871, while consistent with remarks in 1866, tended to emphasize a congressional grant of power that they had played down in 1866. This shifting in argument is characterization of positions taken in later civil rights debate.

Michael C. Kerr argued that the Fourteenth Amendment conferred no power upon Congress to protect the guarantees of section one. The privileges and immunities clause related to rights following only from United States citizenship as defined in Article Four, section two, of the Constitution and did not involve rights pertaining to state citizenship. Congress therefore overstepped itself when it sought to protect rights solely within state jurisdiction, said Kerr. The due process of law clause restated what was already in the Constitution, he continued, except that states now must also not deprive anyone of life, liberty, or property without due process of law. Also, the equal protection of the laws clause granted no power to Congress since it was simply "declaratory of the preexisting law of the country." [36] The contrast between these remarks and those by Kerr in 1866 is to be noted. In 1866 he had attacked proposals to guarantee civil rights because they generally were invading state power within that field and specifically would give Congress power to integrate the schools.[37]

John F. Farnsworth also opposed the bill and introduced a controversy regarding the contrast between Bingham' a amendment of February, 1866, and the Fourteenth Amendment. The former contained a congressional grant of power, said Farnsworth, while the Fourteenth Amendment did not.[38] As has been noted in the previous chapter, Bingham denied this interpretation and stated the Fourteenth Amendment was more comprehensive than his February amendment. The Ohio representative then gave a lengthy defense of the bill as one giving federal protection to the rights guaranteed by the Bill of Rights.[39] Henry L. Dawes and. Henry Wilson both supported Bingham's interpretation in general remarks upon the bill.[40]

James A. Garfield agreed with Farnsworth, that the Amendment was not so powerful as the February proposal. The future President did feel, however, that Congress had the power to enforce the limitation of state power expressed in the equal protection of the laws clause. He would support the bill, he stated, if the offenses of the Ku Klux Klan were clearly indicated, if it were made clear that Congress did not have original jurisdiction in the guarantee of rights, and if the provisions to suspend the writ of *habeas corpus* and to declare martial law were eliminated from the bill.[41]

Lyman Trumbull agreed generally with the aim of the bill but disagreed with Radical interpretation of the Fourteenth Amendment. He argued that the only "new provision" in the Amendment was the equal protection of the laws clause (upon which he offered no comment). The privileges and immunities clause was no stronger than Article Four, section two, he stated. He felt the Amendment neither conferred upon Congress any more power than it had had before 1866 nor extended the rights belonging to United States citizenship that had existed prior to

1866. The Amendment merely extended that guarantee to a new class, he said, which was the Negro.[42]

George F. Edmunds and Matthew H. Carpenter of Wisconsin (Rep.) disagreed with Trumbull. Edmunds believed that prior to the Fourteenth. Amendment rights stemming from United States citizenship were dependent upon state citizenship, whereas now all states must respect rights pertaining to a national citizenship that preceded state citizenship. Carpenter noted that Congress now had power to secure the rights of United States citizenship, whereas previously protection had been left to the courts. In reply to the latter argument Trumbull noted that by the necessary and, proper clause of the original constitution Congress was given the power to enforce the negative prohibitions upon the exercise of state power; the Fourteenth Amendment was simply a restatement of this original design, he said. Carpenter said that he had never heard of that construction of the Constitution. If it were true, he added, certainly no amendment could give Congress any more power. At any rate, Carpenter concluded, the interpretation "is satisfactory for all purposes of this bill." Trumbull finally voted against the bill because of objection to part of the provisions for enforcement.[43]

Those participating in debate on this bill who had not been members of the first session of the Thirty-ninth Congress generally offered the same sort of defense or opposition to the bill as the others. Horatio C. Burchard of Illinois (Rep.), for example, presented the same interpretation of the Fourteenth Amendment to the House that Trumbull had given to the Senate.[44]

Senators Morton and Frelinghuysen defended the Radical interpretation of the Amendment in the Senate. A negative prohibition was the same as an "affirmative provision," said. Norton. [45] Frelinghuysen believed the privileges and immunities clause more comprehensive than Article Four, section two. The former defined United States citizenship and expressed a guarantee of privileges and immunities pertaining to that status. "The highest privilege of a man is the formation of character," said Frelinghuysen, and the most comprehensive privilege is the pursuit of happiness. The New Jersey Senator also referred to rights enumerated in Corfield V. Coryell. In concluding remarks the Senator stated: "A State denies equal protection whenever it fails to give it. Denying includes inaction as well as action."[46]

In opposition to the bill Senator Thurman of Ohio noted that there was no definition of privileges and immunities in the bill. If Sumner's civil rights bill became law, he continued, all men who did not allow Negroes and whites to mix in hotels, steamboats, railways, schools, inns, churches, and places of public amusement would be liable for punishment under the terms of the bill.

There was just this one major discussion of the Fourteenth Amendment between 1866 and 1872, and comments generally were related only to the question of whether state or federal government was to assume responsibility for the protection of rights guaranteed by the Amendment. There was little discussion of the scope of the Amendment's guarantee at this time, except for Thurman's reference to Sumner's civil rights bill.

Other references to the Fourteenth Amendment during this period, while few, are significant, for they provide an early interpretation of the Amendment with regard to Negro education. As previously noted, both Frelinghuysen and Stewart expressed their belief that the Amendment would require the states to make provision for Negro education, and in such a manner as to prevent any kind of discrimination. Senator Howe had also expressed this thought in 1866 in defense of the Amendment itself. Frelinghuysen believed the states were left free to determine whether or not schools were to be integrated. Rowe and Stewart, on the other hand, in later civil rights debate, expressed their belief that the Fourteenth Amendment enabled Congress to require integration, although neither felt it was necessary to do so.

Conservative opposition to Radical efforts during this period expressed a characteristic fear that integrated schools would, result from endeavors to guarantee equality and from efforts to make provision for Negro education. And to construct a defense against this fear Senator Henderson tried unsuccessfully to gain Senate endorsement of the separate but equal doctrine. This same type of defense emerged later in Conservative opposition to the various civil rights bills of the 1870s.

It must be repeated, however, that these references to the Fourteenth Amendment with regard to Negro education and these Conservative comments regarding integration, while significant, are not characteristic of discussions about Negro education during the five year period between 1866 and. 1872. Most of the remarks about Negro education were made with reference to the Negro's need to be educated because of his new status within society, and particular emphasis was given to his need for education because of his being granted the suffrage.

The extension of the suffrage, in fact, along with Radical efforts to establish state governments under their control, was the predominate aspect of reconstruction legislation during this period. Concern for Negro education seems only to have stemmed from this main effort, and Congress was willing to leave the states to settle for themselves the question of whether schools would be segregated or integrated. There was, for the most part, a distinction between comments related to the guarantee of civil equality and comments related to Negro education.

This distinction disappeared, however, when, in 1872, Congress became embroiled in debate over a civil rights bill that sought to integrate the schools.

FOOTNOTES: CHAPTER II

1. December 18, 1865, <u>Congressional Globe</u>, 39 Cong., 1 sess., I, 67; February 7, 1866, <u>Ibid</u>., I, 708-712; May 21, 1866, <u>Ibid</u>., III, 2719; July 18, 1866, <u>Ibid</u>., V, 3906; July 27, 1866, <u>Ibid</u>., V, 4278; March 3, 1868, <u>Congressional Globe</u>, 40 Cong., 2 sess., II, 1621; March 20, 1868, <u>Ibid</u>., II. 2028: July 10, 1868, <u>Ibid</u>., IV, 3900.

   Provision had been made by Congress in 1862 and 1864 for the establishment of Negro schools. Originally these schools were to be supported by taxes levied upon the Negroes themselves for the purpose, and then later they were to be supported by an amount from the general school fund proportionate to the ratio of Negro to white children. No schools had been established by 186$, however, because of insufficient funds. In 1865 one Negro school was constructed, and by the end of the school year in 1867 there were five. George F. T. Cook, "Historical Sketch of the Colored Schools, Past and Present," <u>First Report of the Board of Trustees of Public Schools in the District of Columbia 1874-'75</u> (Washington: McGill and Witherow, 1876), 9345.

2. January 10, 1870, <u>Congressional Globe</u>, 41 Cong., 2 sess., I, 323; February 8, 1871, <u>Congressional Globe</u>, 41 Cong., 3 sess., II, 1050-1061; December 12, 1511, <u>Congressional Globe</u>, 2 Cong., 2 sess., I, 68; December 11, 1872, <u>Congressional Globe</u>, 42 Cong. 3 sess., I, 123; December 4, 1863,73, <u>Congressional Record</u>, 13 Cong., 1 sess., I, 57.

3. Discussion of the District of Columbia school integration bill occurred in 1871. There was no direct reference to the Fourteenth Amendment, but it is obvious that Sumner felt integration necessary if there were to be equality before the law.

   The bill of 1871 and other like it failed ever to come to a vote. February 8, 1871, <u>Congressional Globe</u>, 41 Cong., 3 sess., II, 1054, 1055-1056.

4. Between 1866 and 1869 Sumner had introduced and secured the passage of legislation aimed at the destruction of distinctions made because of color in voting, holding office, and serving as a juror. December 3, 1866, <u>Congressional Globe</u>, 39 Cong., 2 sess., I, 2; July 19, 1867, <u>Congressional Globe</u>, 40 Cong., 1 sess., 727; January 24, 1868, <u>Congressional Globe</u>, 40 Cong., 2 sess., I, 720; March 3, 1869, Congressional Globe, 40 Cong., 3 sess. III, 1826; March 17, 1869, Congressional Globe, 41 Cong., 1 sess., 125.

    Prior to 1866 Sumner had also secured the legal destruction of discrimination made because of color on the street railways and in the selection of witnesses in court.
5. January 16, 1867, <u>Congressional Globe</u>, 39 Cong., 2 sess., I, 504; January 28, 1867 <u>Ibid.</u>, I, 816.
6. January 3, 1867, <u>Ibid.</u>, I, 253. Ashley had voted for the Fourteenth Amendment in 1866.
7. March 7 1867, <u>Congressional Globe</u>, 40 Cong., 1 sess., 15.
8. March 11, 1867, <u>Ibid.</u>, 50.
9. March 11, 1867, <u>Ibid.</u>, 52, 56.
10. March 12, 1867, <u>Ibid.</u>, 70-71.
11. March 12, 1867, <u>Ibid.</u>, 69. <u>Documents of the General Assembly of Indiana at The Forty Fifth Regular Session</u> (Indianapolis: Samuel N. Douglass, 1867), I, 21, 25-21.
12. March 16, 1867, <u>Congressional Globe</u>, 10 Cong., 1 sess., 165.
13. March 16, 1867, <u>Ibid.</u>, 168.
14. March 16, 1867, <u>Ibid.</u>, 168, 170.
15. March 16, 1867, Ibid., 169.
16. March 16, 1867, <u>Ibid.</u>, 167, 169.
17. July 11, 1867, <u>Ibid.</u>, 581.
18. July 16, 1867, <u>Ibid.</u>, 625.
19. May 30, 1868, <u>Congressional Globe</u>, 40 Cong., 2 sess., III, 2701. Henderson had voted for the Fourteenth Amendment in 1866.
20. <u>Loc. cit.</u>; June 1, 1868, <u>Ibid.</u>, III, 2747-2748.

21. June 1, 1868, <u>Ibid.</u>, III, 2748.

22. June 5, 1868, <u>Ibid.</u>, III, 2858; June 10, 1868, <u>Ibid.</u>, III, 3013.

23. February 14, 1870, <u>Congressional Globe</u>, 41 Cong., 2 sess., I, 1253-1254.

24. January 21, 1870, <u>Ibid.</u>, I, 637; January 24, 1870, <u>Ibid.</u>, I, 716-717.

25. February 16, 1870, <u>Ibid.</u>, II, 1329.

26. May 22, 1874, <u>Congressional Record</u>, 43 Cong., 1, sess., V., 4167.

27. December 18, 1868, <u>Congressional Globe,</u> 40 Cong., 2 sess., V, "Appendix" 70.

28. May 8, 1868, <u>Ibid.</u>, III, 2395; February 11, 1870, <u>Congressional Globe,</u> 41 Cong., 2 sess., II, 1218.

29. June 8, 1866, <u>Congressional Globe</u>, 39 Cong., 1 sess., IV, 304.

30. June 5, 1866, <u>Ibid.</u>, IV, 2966-2967.

31. February 26, 1867, <u>Congressional Globe</u>, 39 Cong., 2 sess., III, 1843.

32. February 7, 1871, <u>Congressional Globe</u>, Cong., 3 sess., II, 1042; February 6, 1872, <u>Congressional Globe</u>, 1.2 Cong., 2 sess., I, 854, 860, 861. Dawes had been in Congress in 1866; the others had not.

33. February 2, 1872,<u> Ibid.</u>, I, 788-789, 791-792; February 6, 1872, <u>Ibid.</u>, I, 855-856.

34. February 6, 1872, <u>Ibid.</u>, I, 856.

35. March 23, 1871, <u>Congressional Globe</u>, 12 Cong., 1 sess., I, 236; March 28, 1871, <u>Ibid.</u>, I, 17; March 28, 1871, <u>Ibid.</u>, II, "Appendix," 69.

36. March 28, 1871, Ibid., II, "Appendix," 47-48.

37. Supra, I, 14. Kerr voted against the Amendment in 1866.

38. March 31, 1871, Ibid., II, "Appendix," 115-116.

39. <u>Supra</u>, I, 25-27.

40. April 5, 1871, <u>Ibid.</u>, I, 475-476; April 13, 1871, <u>Ibid.</u>, II,"Appendix," 256.

41. April 4, 1871, <u>Ibid.</u>, II, "Appendix," 150-154, Garfield voted for the Amendment in 1866.

42. April 11, 1871, <u>Ibid</u>., I, 575-578; April 14, 1871, <u>Ibid</u>., II, 692-693, 696-697, 709.

43. <u>Loc. cit</u>. Carpenter had not been a member of Congress in 1866. He was elected in 1868. Both Trumbull and Edmunds had voted for the Amendment in 1866. Trumbull's argument in 1871 was characteristic of his "moderate" position in 1866.

44. April 6, 1871, <u>Ibid</u>., II, "Appendix," 315.

45. April 4, 1871, <u>Ibid</u>., II, "Appendix," 251.

46. April 6, 1871, Ibid., I, 500-502.

47. April 13, 1871, <u>Ibid</u>., II, "Appendix," 216-217. The enforcement bill finally passed Congress April 19, 1871 (<u>Ibid</u>., II, 831).

CHAPTER 3

CONGRESS: 1872-1875

S umner first introduced his civil rights bill May 13, 1870. It was reported adversely by the Committee on the Judiciary. He reintroduced it January 20, 1871, and again the Committee reported it adversely. He met failure again when his bill, reintroduced March 3, 1871, died in committee. On December 20, 1871, he by-passed the Committee by moving the entire bill as an amendment of addition to the pending bill to remove the political and legal disabilities administered by the Fourteenth Amendment. Between December 1871 and March 1875 there were three separate civil rights bills that were considered by Congress, two from the Senate and one from the House. The House bill was the one finally adopted in 1875, although all three were essentially the same in scope.

Concurrent with the consideration of these civil rights bills was the renewed conflict between Northern and Southern interests in Congress. Beginning in 1871 a few Southerners again sat in Congress, and they returned in increasing numbers after the passage, in 1872, of a bill removing the political disabilities administered by the Fourteenth Amendment. Civil rights debate, then, was inextricably a part of the political struggle between Radical and Conservative elements. Sumner himself, however, while helping to lead. Radical efforts to keep control of Congress, seems also genuinely to have been concerned with securing for the Negro equality before the law. Several times there were opportunities to pass a modified civil rights bill, and it is likely that Sumner could easily have secured the passage of a token bill that would have been sufficient for use in an appeal for votes. The Senator, however, until his death in 1874, was adamant in his demand for a fully recognized equality before the law. Also, this later effort was entirely consistent with ardent efforts throughout his life aimed first at abolition and then at the guarantee of civil equality for the Negro.

He defended the Thirteenth Amendment as a measure that would destroy all aspects of slavery to bring about an equality before the law. Through the first session of the Thirty-ninth Congress he introduced numerous bills and resolutions designed to enforce the guarantees of the Thirteenth Amendment, referring specifically to both education and the elective franchise as inherent aspects of reconstruction efforts to elevate the status of the Negro. In. 1867 he reemphasized the need to provide for Negro education without distinction of race or color. In 1869, when discussing the Fifteenth Amendment, he suggested broadening it to include all rights since the consideration of a constitutional amendment implied that Congress did not consider the Fourteenth Amendment powerful enough to secure all Negro rights.[2] During the war and. until 1874 Sumner also led efforts to secure Negro rights in the District of Columbia, and then between 1870 and 1874 he initiated and defended national civil rights legislation. The Senator later spoke of the District of Columbia as an "experimental garden" -- "the place where all the great reforms born of the war have begun."[3]

In correspondence and speeches outside Congress Sumner also defended Negro equality. Writing of President Johnson's veto of the civil rights bill in 1866 Sumner addressed the Duchess of Argyll. "The loss of this bill will be a terrible calamity," be declared.

"It leaves the new crop of black laws in full force, and gives to the old masters a new letter of license to do anything with the freedmen short of making him a chattel.[4] In October, 1866, Sumner spoke in Boston in defense of the Fourteenth Amendment and congressional reconstruction. The Amendment, he said, was good as far as it went, but more needed to be done. The Senator then suggested granting the elective franchise to the Negro and giving the Negro a homestead and an education.

In a letter to the Border State Convention at Baltimore during the fall of 1867 Sumner expressed the same thoughts: Congress will leave undone what it ought to do, if it fails to provide for the establishment of Equal Rights, whether political or civil, everywhere throughout the Union."[6] Again at Boston, in a speech October 15, 1870, Sumner called attention to the fact that the whole work of Reconstruction and the establishment of Equal Rights" was disputed by the Democrats. "So long as anybody assails the Declaration of Independence," said the Senator, "the Republican party cannot cease its patriotic labors."[7] And in 1871 he specifically defended integrated schools in a letter to the president of the school board of Jefferson, Texas. The Senator noted what he had stated in 1849 when defending integration before the Massachusetts supreme court, that Negro equality existed only in attending school with whites, and not in schools separate from them.[8]

Of those defending Radical efforts prior to 1872 only Howe and Stewart, in addition to Sumner, had given any hint that the civil rights debate of 1872-1875 might develop.

When defending the Fourteenth Amendment in 1866 Howe had criticized a Florida law whereby whites and Negroes were not equal before the law, and in 1870 Stewart had expressed the opinion that the Fourteenth Amendment enabled Congress to require Southerners to educate the Negro without distinction of color or race.

Democratic opposition to Radical efforts prior to 1872 had also foreshadowed the possibility of later agitation for the guarantee of civil rights. Several, in fact, had pointed to the possibility that Radicals in Congress would require schools to be integrated.

Most congressmen, however, had seemed concerned only with the immediate object of consideration, and the comments of some also reveal that later civil rights legislation was not contemplated prior to the time Sumner introduced his national civil rights bill. Stevens had referred only generally to Negro rights other than the elective franchise, and his efforts had centered more specifically in programs designed to keep the South "loyal." Frelinghuysen had said Sumner's educational reconstruction requirement of 1867 unnecessary. It is true he had expressed the opinion at this time that the Fourteenth Amendment and education were related, but he had felt the states were free to determine for themselves how the Negro would be educated. John Sherman also had opposed Sumner's educational proposal of 1867. He had called it a "mere theoretical proposition" and had said the education of Negroes and, whites was solely within state jurisdiction. And in 1869, in debate on the Fifteenth Amendment, Boutwell had referred to the Amendment as the last "of a series of great measures growing out of the rebellion."[9]

If this later civil rights debate was prompted by Sumner alone, however, and if he had always been concerned with the condition of the Negro, why did he wait until 1870 to introduce his bill? Perhaps he had expected other reconstruction measures to secure the guarantees of the bill and introduced it when it became apparent they would not. He had said, in fact, that he believed the Thirteenth Amendment contained all the power necessary to destroy all aspects of slavery to establish equality before the law. Perhaps, on the other hand, this bill simply followed reconstruction measures that had been considered more important at the time.

In. 1867, for example, he had been willing to let the integration question pass in order to fulfill the immediate need to make some kind of provision for Negro education. It may be he also timed the introduction of his bill in accordance with political efforts to keep Congress in control of Radical hands. Whatever his particular thoughts, however, and regardless of political plans, the Senator was also concerned at this time that Negroes were not enjoying the full privileges incident to equality before the law.

Section one of the bill Sumner first introduced in 1870 sought to guarantee equal and impartial enjoyment of any accommodation, advantage, facility, or privilege furnished by public carriers, inn-keepers, theaters, "or other places of public amusement, schools, churches, cemeteries, and "benevolent institutions." By section four the right to serve as a juror was guaranteed, and by section five any law, statute, or ordinance that created a discrimination of color by the use of the word "white" was declared to be repealed and annulled.[10]

There was opposition from both parties to the inclusion of churches, because of feelings regarding church and state, and this part of the bill was soon dropped.[11] Throughout the evening and morning of May 21-22, 1872, while Sumner was absent, Senator Carpenter almost secured the adoption of a substitute bill that did not include reference to schools, cemeteries, juries, or benevolent institutions.[12] Sumner reintroduced his bill at each session of Congress after its initial consideration in 1872. Before the bill was passed, however, the Senator died (March 11, 1874). When finally adopted by Congress the bill included reference only to inns, public conveyances, theaters "and other places of public amusement," and jury service. The school clause was dropped in February, 1875.

Between 1874 and 1875 a major part of the time spent in discussing Sumner's bill centered in its provision to prevent discrimination in the schools, and there were two attempts in the Senate to clear the uncertainty in the bill with regard to integration. The school provision had clearly required integration when the bill was under Sumner's surveillance but had, been changed in committee after Sumner's death in such a way as to dodge the integration question.

During another meeting of the Senate that lasted all night Boutwell moved to change the wording of the bill in order to make clear its demand for integrated schools. This motion was defeated 5-42, 26 absent.[13] Aaron A. Sargent of California (Rep.), on the other hand, moved to add to the bill the proviso that a state had the right to establish "separate schools ...equal in all respects to others of the same grade." This was moved in two different forms during the same night meeting and was twice defeated, 21-26, and 16-28.[14]

The bill that finally became law originated in the House in December, 1873, and was framed so as to require integration. Because of opposition to this requirement, however, the bill was changed in committee to include a recognition of the establishment of separate schools...giving equal educational advantages."[15] There was opposition to this Jim Crow feature, however, and Stephen W. Kellogg of Connecticut (Rep.), who criticized this recognition of color discrimination and who also felt the federal government had no business legislating in the field of education, moved to strike from the bill all that related to schools. This motion was accepted 128-48,[16] so that the civil rights bill as finally adopted by both houses contained no reference to schools.

Debate on this civil rights legislation was initiated by remarks between Sumner and Lot N. Morrill of Maine, and their discussions centered in comments concerning the power conferred upon Congress by the Fourteenth Amendment.

In his initial speech in defense of his bill Sumner spoke generally of "human rights," and except for references to the Declaration of Independence and the 1866 Civil Rights Act there was no legal" argument. The bill, he explained, was the "complement" of the 1866 act and was necessary to protect all persons fully in their "civil rights." The Senator's appeal was for a full equality before the law, which included integrated public carriers, schools, churches, and other institutions. The "equivalent" in a separate institution, even if the same, was not the equal of the original, claimed Sumner in language practically identical to that used in 1849 before the Massachusetts supreme court. "The substitute is invariably an inferior article...in the process of substitution the vital elixir exhales and escapes. It is lost and cannot be recovered; for Equality is found only in Equality."[17]

A few days later, in answer to Morrill, who had attacked the bill, Sumner more specifically spoke of constitutional issues. "...the Constitution is full of power; it is overrunning with power. I find it not in one place or in two places or three places, but I find it almost everywhere, from the preamble to the last line of the last amendment." The Constitution, insisted the Senator, must be interpreted in light of the Declaration of Independence, for it was of "equal and coordinate authority with the Constitution itself."

Sumner relied specifically upon the Thirteenth Amendment as a measure that completely abolished slavery: "...the article abolishes slavery entirely, everywhere throughout this country. It abolishes it root and branch. It abolishes it in the general and in the particular. It abolishes it in length and breadth and then in every detail."

Sumner continued: "Were I not profoundly convinced that the conclusion founded on the thirteenth amendment was unanswerable, so as to make further discussion surplusage, I should take up the fourteenth amendment and show how, in the first place, we have there the definition of a citizen of the United States, and then in the second place, an inhibition upon the States, so that they cannot make or enforce any law which shall abridge the privileges or immunities of citizens of the United States; nor deny to any person within its jurisdiction the equal protection of the laws, And here again Congress is empowered to enforce these provisions by appropriate legislation. Surely, if there were any doubt in the thirteenth amendment, as there is not, it would be all removed by this supplementary amendment.[18]

Senator Morrill had said in his speech of opposition that the citizenship clause of the Fourteenth Amendment stated nothing that was not already true because of the Thirteenth Amendment. If it were otherwise, the 1866 Civil Rights Act could not possibly be constitutional, he claimed. The privileges and immunities clause and the due process of law clause granted no more rights than were contained in Article Four, section two, of the Constitution, said Morrill. He made no comment upon the equal protection of the laws clause and went on to say that the Fourteenth Amendment only prohibited the states from acting to deprive rights and was not a 'substantive grant of power' to Congress. "Matters of education, worship, amusement, recreation, entertainment,"-- all belonged exclusively to the State, he concluded.[19]

The ensuing discussions involved comments related both to the question of the power conferred upon Congress by the Fourteenth Amendment and to the question of the scope of the equality guaranteed by it. Arguments centered around the privileges and immunities clause, although there were also some remarks about the equal protection of the laws clause.

The opposition tended to emphasize their belief that the Fourteenth Amendment was simply a prohibition upon state authority and did not give Congress the power to legislate in areas reserved to the states. As for education, it was a privilege stemming from state citizenship and not from federal citizenship, they said. Education, therefore, was not a field within which the federal government could legislate, they concluded. And in an effort to weaken the Radical demand for equality the opposition also claimed that equal school privileges in separate schools fulfilled any requirement for equal rights.

Those defending the civil rights bill, on the other hand, claimed the Fourteenth Amendment did provide Congress with the power to enforce its guarantee of equality. It was further stated that the rights enumerated within the bill were privileges incident to United States citizenship and as such were within the realm of congressional Jurisdiction.

There was a division of opinion among those defending the bill with regard to the question of integration. Some felt separate schools would not be a violation of the equality guaranteed by the Fourteenth Amendment while others believed segregation would fall short of that equality. Others simply said that congressional legislation should contain no recognition of segregation but on the other hand should not require integration.

There is an interesting shift in Conservative and Radical arguments between 1866 and 1872. In the 1872 civil rights bill, former Democratic fears materialized--a Radical measure sought to integrate the schools. In 1866, however, advocates of civil rights legislation had denied this interpretation of their efforts, even though they had admitted a change in the balance of power between state and federal government. Conservative opposition in 1872, on the other hand, denied the existence of a congressional power to enforce a guarantee of civil equality, whereas in 1866 they had declared this power to be an inherent aspect of civil rights legislation.

There are exceptions to these various patterns of thought, but they are characteristic of comments made in this later civil rights debate.

One of the leaders of the opposition between 1872 and 187 was Senator Allen O. Thurman, and his argument contained ideas expressed by several others at this time. The Senator claimed the Fourteenth Amendment did not section protection of privileges and immunities unless the state had denied any of them to its citizens. The bill, therefore, illegally sought to regulate rights before any deprivation had, occurred. The bill was related only to the privileges and immunities clause, explained Thurman, so that the due process of law clause was irrelevant, and the equal protection of the laws clause was also of no importance in the question because it was related only to the rights of life, liberty, and property.

If there were deprivation of right under the privileges and immunities clause, claimed the Senator, then recourse was through the courts and not through Congress. He also believed the bill was aimed not at the state, but at individuals--owners of inns, theaters, railroads, "and the like."[20]

Thurman defended the state right to regulate the school system and said that if separation of the sexes were legal under the Fourteenth Amendment, so was separation of the races. The "equal protection of the laws" required only equal facilities, he said.[21] The Senator then noted later in debate that by an Ohio supreme court decision, The State of Ohio ex rel. William Garnes v. John W. McCann (1872), the constitutionality of segregated schools had been upheld upon consideration of the Fourteenth Amendment.[22]

It was from the Supreme Court's decision in the Slaughter House Case that Thurman and others of similar thought later drew additional support for their position. The argument then became set in the distinction noted in the decision between the privileges and immunities pertaining to United States citizenship and those related to state citizenship. Thus Thurman stated: "It is not provided that no State shall make or enforce any law which shall abridge the privileges and immunities of citizens of the United States 'or of the State.' There are no such words as 'or of the State.' It is only a limitation on the power of the State to make a law which shall abridge the privileges and immunities of citizens of the United States and leaves the State to deal with its citizens as it has the power to do in regard to their privileges and immunities as citizens of the State."[23]

Among the many[24] that opposed Sumner's civil rights bill were two, in addition to Morrill, that had been members of the first session of the Thirty-ninth Congress. Senator Garrett Davis and William E. Fink of Ohio (Dem.) expressed sentiments similar to those uttered by Thurman and others of the opposition. Davis stated the Fourteenth Amendment conferred no power upon

Congress and expressed his belief that remedy for violation of its terms was through the Courts.[25] Fink referred to the Slaughter House decision and to The State of Ohio ex rel. William Garnes v. John W. McCann in his opposition to the bill.[26]

Most of the opposition confined their remarks to the question of the constitutionality of the bill. Several, however, along with Thurman, also tried to weaken Radical argument by claiming that equal provision for separate schools fulfilled any requirement for equality before the law.

Senator John W. Johnston of Virginia (Dem.) spoke of an equal Negro share of the school money and of equal school houses for the two groups.[27] Senator John P. Stockton of New Jersey (Dem.) believed the Fourteenth Amendment guaranteed the Negro "a right to precisely as good accommodations and equal accommodations" in schools as those for white children. By seeking integration, however, the bill was trying to make Negroes "superior to the law," he claimed.[28] Aylett H. Buckner of Missouri (Dem.) also said the bill sought not "equality of right," but "identity of right" in requiring integration, and. Lewis V. Bogy of Missouri (Dem.) referred to the Negro's "equal share of the benefits" of the school system.[29] Senator Augustus S. Merriman of North Carolina (Dem.) defined the equal protection of the laws clause of the Fourteenth Amendment to mean "the same measure of protection of the law." It did not mean, he contended, that the state could not "regulate the exercise of rights of one sort or another." He then spoke in defense of separate schools.[30]

Two Republicans, who were in sympathy with the aim of the bill, also opposed the effort to integrate the schools. Alexander White of Alabama defended "equal rights and separate enjoyment" as a matter of "expediency," and Senator Aaron A. Sargent of California believed that if the Fourteenth Amendment required an equal education to be extended to all people of the country without regard to color then separate schools fulfilled that requirement.[31]

The Conservative defense of equal rights in separate schools seems in itself to be a concession to Radical power, for it admits a tie between the Fourteenth Amendment's requirement for equality and the field of education, whereas formerly this relationship was not recognized by those opposing efforts to guarantee civil equality.

Radicals differed in their opinions concerning integration, on the other hand, but were united in their insistence that the various civil rights bills were constitutional.

A few of those defending the constitutionality of the civil rights bill drew support for their stand from the Slaughter House decision. There were remarks about the brief comments of the decision related to the equal protection of the laws clause and about the general statements related to the purpose of the civil war amendments. Freylinghuysen and Morton believed this clause to be aimed at the destruction of the discrimination that followed because of slavery.[32] Senator Rowe also quoted from the Slaughter House decision in a defense of the civil rights bill, as did Robert B. Elliott of South Carolina (Negro, Rep.) and John R. Lynch of Mississippi (Negro, Rep.).[33]

There were others, on the other hand, who, in order to discount the claim of Southern support from the Supreme Court decision, stated the opinions of the justices were either in error or not relevant to the present question. Boutwell argued that there was no distinction between the privileges and immunities of citizens of the United States and citizens of the state. Because of the Fourteenth Amendment, he explained, the first "immunity" and privilege of a citizen of the United States was his equality with any other citizen within the state. The state, therefore, could make no distinction among the citizens of the United States residing within the state, he said. Boutwell later stated that states had the power to say what privileges and immunities would be conferred upon its citizens but also noted that no distinction could be made in the administration of a privilege granted, because as citizens of the United States all persons were equal before the law.[34] John H. Lynch felt the Slaughter House decision as used by the opposition irrelevant since the case involved discrimination not involving race, color, or previous condition of servitude. Boutwell also drew this distinction between the scope of the Court decision and that of the Amendment.[35]

Others[36] defending the civil rights bill spoke either of the right to be educated *per se* or the right to be educated with whites as a right guaranteed by the privileges and immunities clause of the Fourteenth Amendment. Senator Matthew H. Carpenter of Wisconsin believed all the rights enumerated in the bill, except those related to churches and jurors, were secured by the privileges and immunities clause. He noted the difference between Article Four, section two, of the Constitution and. the Fourteenth Amendment. By the former a citizen of one state moving to another did not carry with him the rights granted by the first state. By the Fourteenth Amendment, on the other hand, a citizen in any state would be guaranteed the privileges and immunities belonging to citizens of the United States, he said. With particular emphasis the Wisconsin Senator defended education as a right included within the scope of the Amendment.[37]

Senator Sherman also referred to the Negro's "right to go to the common schools" under the privileges and immunities clause.[38] Frelinghuysen admitted the Fourteenth Amendment did not require the granting of any of the privileges enumerated in the bill, but, he said, there must be no discrimination in the administration of those privileges when granted.[39] Howe claimed. Congress now had "supreme jurisdiction" in the question of declaring what were and what were not privileges and. immunities. This jurisdiction the states had relinquished with the civil war amendments, he said, and if they had not, he noted, then the 1866 Civil Rights Act would be unconstitutional.[40]

One other aspect of the defense of the constitutionality of this legislation was an emphasis upon the power conferred by section five of the Fourteenth Amendment. Morton explained that while the Amendment granted no new privileges and immunities, it did grant power to Congress to enforce the equality demanded by it.[41] Boutwell, Carpenter, and Robert S. Hale of New York also interpreted section five as one granting Congressional power, and Hale noted his opposition to the Amendment when it had been before Congress in 1866. He had opposed it, he explained, just because it <u>was</u> a "revolution" in the form of government.[42]

Those defending the constitutionality of the civil rights bill were divided in their opinion regarding the question of integration. Eight either spoke in favor of integration or said they did not care to have legislation recognize segregation. Of these eight four had been members of the first session of the Thirty-ninth Congress -- Sumner, Sherman, Boutwell, and Howe -- all of whom referred to the Fourteenth Amendment in their defense of the bill.

Sumner and Boutwell were the only ones that unconditionally supported integrated schools as a requirement of the equality expressed in the Fourteenth Amendment. Sumner felt separate schools were substitutes for equality; even if accommodations are the same, as notoriously they are not, there is no Equality." Boutwell echoed Sumner's condemnation of segregation; "Equal facilities" in "different schools" would "rot" the system of public education.[43]

Sherman believed the bill did not require integration, but, he noted with reference to schools in Ohio, integration was a satisfactory arrangement when prior consent had been reached by the parents concerned.[44] Howe also believed the bill did not require schools to be integrated. He said, however, that he preferred that they be integrated, and he thought such a requirement would be constitutional. What he did not want was a recognition of segregation within the bill, since this would mean that Negroes would have to take 'just such accommodations as are provided, let them be poor or good."[45] Frelinghuysen also felt the bill did not require schools to be integrated. He believed a choice by each person between schools that provided "equal privileges" would be legal. He, too, however, did not want legislation to recognize segregated schools, because those for Negroes would be "inferior to those for the whitey and because the recognition itself would perpetuate a "lingering prejudice."[46]

Three of those defending the civil rights bill either did not speak in defense of integration or seemed to favor Segregation. These men were Stewart, who had been a member of Congress in 1866, Richard H. Cain of South Carolina (Negro, Rep.), and Morton, who had entered Congress after 1866. Senator Stewart believed the bill clearly should not require schools to be integrated, even though he thought such a requirement would be constitutional. He felt the states should be left free to determine whether their schools would be segregated or integrated and seemed himself to favor segregation.[47] Cain asked for legislation that would at least keep the states from depriving Negroes of an education *per se*. He did not express himself with regard to the segregation issue.

Morton evidently preferred that schools be separate. His remarks in 1867 as governor of Indiana support segregation, and his defense of the civil rights bill in 1874, while not altogether clear, seems to indicate the same preference.[49]

The remaining seven that spoke of the constitutionality of the civil rights bill either gave no indication of their opinion concerning segregation or referred to the question in ambiguous language. Robert B. Elliott, William Lawrence, and Robert S. Hale said nothing of the issue. Lawrence and. Hale had been members of the Thirty-ninth Congress. Of those whose stand is not clear only Edmunds had been present in Congress when the Fourteenth Amendment was framed. At one point Edmunds defended integration; at another, he voted against an amendment to the bill offered by Boutwell that clearly would have required integration.

It is evident, however, that he did not desire the civil rights bill to recognize segregation.[50]

Others whose stand is not clear are Carpenter, Benjamin F. Butler, and James L. Alcorn. The only certainty in Carpenter's position is his wish not to make a distinction of color in the bill by recognizing segregated schools.[51] Butler shifted about and finally expressed the opinion that it would be better to strike all reference to education from the bill,[52] while Alcorn spoke in defense of integration but voted against Boutwell's amendment that would have required schools to be integrated.[53]

There were, then, varying comments about the segregation issue from those that had been members of the first session of the Thirty-ninth Congress and defended the constitutionality of the civil rights bill between 1872 and 1875. Sumner and Boutwell spoke unconditionally in favor of integration. Sherman and Howe felt the bill did not require integration, but they both were favorable to it. Howe also said there should be no legal recognition of segregation. Stewart believed the states should settle the question of integration for themselves. Edmunds did not care to have the bill recognize segregation, but he did not give a clear indication of his thought regarding integration. Lawrence and Hale, on the other hand, said nothing about the issue.

Sumner's civil rights bill passed the Senate in the morning hours of May 23, 1874, after a continuous session throughout the night.[54] The bill had been altered in committee after Sumner's death in March, so that the school provision did not clearly indicate a call for integration, and there had been efforts to clarify the ambiguity. These attempts were defeated, however, so that schools might have been either segregated or integrated under the terms of the school provision as passed.

In the House the bill remained on the table for the duration of the time spent discussing civil rights. The House considered its own civil rights bill, which had been introduced by Butler December

18, 1873. It was identical to Sumner's bill in its clear demand for integrated institutions.[55] There were two unsuccessful efforts by House members to amend the bill by incorporating requirements for separate facilities.[56] Then on December 16, 1874, in an apparent concession to Conservative arguments, Butler brought the bill from committee with its school provision changed to require "separate schools ...giving equal educational advantages.[57]

On February 3, 1875, Stephen W. Kellogg of Connecticut moved to strike from the bill all that related to schools, and on the same day Alexander White of Alabama (Rep.) offered a substitute bill seeking recognition of segregation in all the various institutions mentioned in the bill.[58] Discussion centered in the Kellogg amendment, and it was approved 128-48 February 14.[59]

It was a legislative recognition of a "distinction in color" that Kellogg criticized. It was, he believed, contrary to the concept of equality before the law. He also opposed the school provision because he believed education to be solely within state jurisdiction.[60] Several others joined Kellogg in his criticism of the bill's requirement for segregated schools and expressed their disapproval of legislation that recognized a "distinction between American citizens and a discrimination" because of race or color.[61]

The House bill passed February 4, 162-99, and was introduced in the Senate on February 6.[62] There was no Senate attempt to reincorporate provision for education. The bill passed the Senate February 27, 1875, after two days of debate, with requirements to prevent discriminations made because of color in inns, public conveyances theaters "and other places of public amusement," and in the selection of jurors.[63]

Here, then, was an effort consistent with former Radical measures designed to elevate the status of the Negro by granting to him, in addition to his freedom, an equality with any other citizen before the law. The Radical concept of the scope of that equality had broadened by 1872, however, since it generally had been denied in 1866 that civil rights legislation would affect areas included in the later civil rights bills. The Democratic opposition had feared Radical efforts in 1866 would cause the integration of the schools, but they also altered their position in 1872 by denying the constitutionality of the pending civil rights bill.

FOOTNOTES: CHAPTER III

1. May 13, 1870, Congressional Globe. Cong., 2 sess., IV, 3434i July 7, 1870, Ibid., 7V, $3i14. January 20, 1871, Congressional Globe, 41 co g., 3 sess., I, 619; February 15, 1871, Ibid. , II, 1263; March 9, 1871, Congressional Globe, 42 Cong., 1 sess., I, 21; December 20, 1871, Congressional Globe, 42 Cong., 2 sess., I, 240.

    George P. Edmunds of the Committee on the Judiciary said later that the Committee had not reported the bill because it had felt it unnecessary. The 1866 Civil Rights Act, he explained in defense of the Committee's action, while defending Sumner's bill had been thought adequate (January 31, 1872, Ibid., I, 731h Edmunds did not explain what he meant by adequate. Frelinghuysen and Matthew H. Carpenter of Wisconsin (Rep.), who were active in support of the 1872 bill, were also members of the Committee.

2. February 8, 1869, Congressional Globe, 40 Cong., 3 sess., II, 1002, 1008, 1012; February 9, 1869, Ibid., II, 1011.

3. Charles Sumner to the Colored Citizens of Washington, July 29, 1873, in Charles Sumner, The Works of Charles Sumner, XV, 275-278.

4. Charles Sumner to the Duchess of Argyll, April 3, 1866, in Edward L. Pierce, Memoir and Letters of Charles Sumner, IV, 275. The Duchess was the niece of Sumner's friend, the seventh Earl of Carlisle, who had died December 5, 1864 (Pierce, op. cit., IV, 261).

5. Charles Sumner, October 2, 1866, The One Man Power vs. Congress! (Boston: Wright and Potter, 1866). (U.S. Political Pamphlets, VII, no. 11, p. 18.)

6. Charles Sumner to the Border State Convention, September 8, 1867, in Charles Sumner, Works, XII, 18k. The convention had convened to advance the cause of Negro suffrage; Sumner was unable to attend.

7. Charles Sumner, October 15, 1870, "The Republican Party: Its Past and. Future Work," in Charles Sumner, op. cit., XIV, 3-4.
8. Charles Sumner to George W. Walker, July 28, 1871, in Charles Sumner, op. cit., XIV, 310.
9. January 23, 1869, <u>Congressional Globe</u>, 10 Cong., 3 sess., I, 555.
10. December 20, 1871, Congressional Globe, 42 Cong., 2 sess., I, 244.
11. February 8, 1872, Ibid., II, 899.
12. May 21, 1872, Ibid., V, 3735. Carpenter's substitute was accepted, but than the Senate became involved in discussion of parliamentary procedure regarding a motion to reconsider Carpenter's substitute. Sumner had been roused from sleep in the meantime and was present for this debate. At 10:20 A.M. a motion to adjourn by John W. Stevenson of Kentucky (Dem.) was accepted, so that the motion to reconsider the substitute did not come to a vote, thus arresting the passage of it (Ibid., V, 3738-3743).
13. May 22, 1874, congressional Record, 43 Cong., 1 sess., v, 4169.
14. May 22, 1874, Ibid., v, 4167-4175.
15. February 3, 1875, Congressional Record, 43 Cong., 2 sess., I, 939.
16. Loc. cit.; February 4, 1875, Ibid., II, 997, 1010.
17. January 15, 1872, Congressional Globe, 42 Cong., 2 sess., I, 381-384.
18. January 31, 1872, Ibid., I, 727-728.
19. January 25, 1872, Ibid., VI, "Appendix," 2-5.
20. January 22, 1872, Ibid., I, 496; February 1, 1872, Ibid., I, 761; May 20, 1871, Congressional Record, 43 Cong., 1 sess., V, 4085.
21. February 6, 1872, Congressional Globe, 42 Cong., 2 sess., VI, Appendix," 26-27.
22. May 20, 1874, Congressional Record, 43 Cong., 1 sess., V, 4088-4089.
23. May 20, 1874, Ibid., V, 4086-4088.

24. Of the thirty-four congressmen that spoke of the unconstitutionality of the civil rights bill thirty were Democrats and four were Republicans. Twenty-four Democrats were from Southern or Border States. The four Republicans were from the North and West. Thurman, from Ohio, had been born and had lived six years in Virginia.

25. February 1, 1872, Congressional Globe, 42 Cong., 2 sess., I, 763-764. Davis had voted against the Fourteenth Amendment in 1866.

26. February 3, 1875, Congressional Record, 43 Cong. 2 sess., II, 948-949. Fink had voted against the Amendment in 1866.

27. May 21, 1974, Congressional Record, 43 Cong., 1 sess., V, 4115.

28. May 22, 1874, Ibid., V, 4144.

29. January 6, 1874, Ibid., 428; May 22, 1874.

30. May 22, 1874, Ibid., VI, "Appendix," 313.

31. February 4, 1875, Congressional Record, 43 Cong., 2 sess., III, "Appendix," 15 White offered a substitute bill designed to keep Negro and white separate, which was defeated 91-114 (February 4, 1875, Ibid., II, 1010).

    May 22, 1874, Congressional Record, 43 Cong., 1 sess., V, 4171-4172. Lot M. Morrill said nothing about the segregation issue in his remarks criticizing the bill but did vote for an amendment to the bill, submitted by Sargent, that recognized segregation (May 22, 1874, Ibid., V, 4167).

32. April 29, 1871, Ibid., IV, 3453-3454; May 21, 1874, Ibid., VI, "Appendix," 358.

33. May 22, 1874, Ibid., V, 4149-4150; January 6, 1874, Ibid., I, 408-410; February 3, 1875, Congressional Record, 43 Cong., 2 sess., II, 944.

    Elliott did not participate in a discussion of integration in the South Carolina Radical constitutional convention of 1868, of which he was a member (Infra, IV, 4LS).

34. May 21, 1874, Congressional Record, 43 Cong., 1 sess., v, 4116; February 26, 1875, Congressional Record, 43 Cong., 2 sess., III, 1793.
35. February 3, 1875, Ibid., II, 943; February 26, 1875, Ibid., III, 1792.
36. The eighteen defending the constitutionality of the civil rights bill were Republicans and were from the North, West, and South.
37. February 1, 1872, Congressional Globe, 42 Cong., 2 sess., I, 762-763. Between 1871 and 1873 Carpenter was a lawyer in cases involving an interpretation of the Fourteenth Amendment. In Bradwell v. The State of Illinois (16 Wallace, 130) Carpenter argued that it was a civil right under the privileges and immunities clause for anyone--black, white, male, female, married, single--to pursue any avocation. Myra Bradwell had been refused admission to the Illinois bar because she was a married woman. The Court did not sustain Carpenter's argument, although Chief Justice Chase did agree with the Senator in a dissenting opinion. In the Slaughter House Case Carpenter, along with Jeremiah S. Black and Thomas J. Durant, was counsel for Louisiana and the Crescent City Company and argued that there had been no violation of the Fourteenth Amendment. Frank A. Flower, Life of Matthew Hale Carpenter (Madison: David Atwood and Company, 1883), 133-135.

Up until 1866 Carpenter had opposed congressional efforts to secure Negro rights and had expressed this belief in correspondence with Charles D. Robinson, editor of the Green Bay Advocate (Charles D. Robinson MSS; Flower, op. cit., 241- 22). On October 4, 1866, however, in a speech at Milwaukee, the Senator defended the Fourteenth amendment and continued to do so until 1875 Matthew Hale carpenter, The Issue before the People (U.S. political pamphlets, XIV, no. 1, p. 8). Then in 1875 Carpenter switched back to his more "conservative" position prior to 1866 by declaring his belief that the pending civil rights bill was unconstitutional (February 27, 1875, Congressional Record, 43 Cong., 2 sess., III, 1861-1862).

38. February 6, 1872, Ibid., I, 844.
39. April 29, 1874, Congressional Record, 43 Cong., 1 sess., IV, 3454.
40. May 22, 1874, Ibid., V, 4150.
41. January 23, 1872, Congressional Globe, 43 Cong., 2 sess., I, 525.
42. May 21, 1874, Congressional Record, 43 Cong., 1 sess., V, 4115; February 1, 1872 Congressional Globe, 12 Cong., 2 sess., I, 762; February 4, 1875, Congressional Record, 43 Cong., 2 sess., II, 979-980.

Hale's explanation of support of the civil rights bill in 1875 was somewhat faulty. He stated at this time that he had opposed the Fourteenth Amendment by voice and vote, whereas actually he had opposed Bingham's February amendment and had voted for the Fourteenth Amendment. It is not clear why he voted for the Fourteenth Amendment. Perhaps he felt, as others later claimed, that the Amendment was not so powerful as Bingham's earlier proposal. Perhaps he had become convinced of the desirability of a change in power relations.

43. January 15, 1872, Congressional Globe, 42 Cong., 2 sess., I, 382-383; May 21, 1874, Congressional Record, 43 Cong., 1 sess., V, 4116,
44. May 8, 1872, Congressional Globe, 42 Cong., 2 sess. IV, 3192-3193.
45. May 22, 1874, Congressional Record, 43 Cong., 1 sess., V, 4150-4151.
46. April 29, 1874, Ibid., IV, 3452.
47. May 22, 1874, Ibid., V, 4167.
48. January 21, 1874, Ibid., 1, 565-566. Cain did not participate in a discussion of integration in the South Carolina Radical

constitutional convention of 1868, of which he was a member (Infra, IV, 145).

49. May 21, 1874, Ibid., IV, "Appendix," 358-359.

50. May 22, 1874, Ibid., V, 4169, 4171-4173

51. May 22, 1874, Ibid., V, 4167.

52. December 18, 1873, Ibid., I, 318; January 2, 1874, Ibid., I,456-457; February 3, 1875, Congressional Record, 43 Cong., 2 sess., II, 939; February 4,1875, Ibid., II, 1005-1006.

53. May 22, 1874, Congressional Record, 43 Cong., 1 sess., VI, "Appendix," 305; May 22, 1874, Ibid., V, 4169.

54. May 22, 1874, Ibid., V, 4175.

55. December 18, 1873, Ibid., I, 318.

56. January 6, 1874, Ibid., I, 405, 407. The two men were James B. Beck of Kentucky and Lloyd Lowndes Jr. of Maryland, both Democrats.

57. December 16, 1874, Congressional Record, 43 Cong., 2 sess., I, 116.

58. February 3, 1875, Ibid., II, 939. White's substitute was defeated 91-114 February 1 (Ibid., II, 1010).

59. February 4, 1875, Ibid., II, 1010.

60. February 4, 1875, Ibid., II, 997•

61. February 4, 187$, Ibid.., II, 997-998, 999-1000, 1002. These men were James Monroe of Ohio (Rep.), Julius C. Burrows of Michigan (Rep.), and Charles O. Williams of Wisconsin (Rep.).

62. February 4, 1875, Ibid., II, 1011; February 6, Ibid., II, 1031.

63. February 26-27, 1875, Ibid., III, 1791-1799, 1861-1870.

The only attempt to broaden the House bill was made by Thomas W. Tipton of Nebraska (Dem.). He unsuccessfully sought to incorporate provision for the prevention of discrimination in churches, "where," he said, "it is supposed that all men stand equal before the divine law." (February 27, 1875, Ibid., III, 1869.)

CHAPTER 4

SUMMARY: CONGRESS: 1866-1875

A few members of the first session of the Thirty-ninth Congress remained in Congress at least until 1872, some until 1875. A resume of their opinions about civil rights legislation and Negro education follows, in order more clearly to indicate the relevancy of the later civil rights debate to the entire question of the intent of the framers of the Fourteenth Amendment with regard to Negro education.

The civil rights bill that Sumner first introduced in 1870 was not totally unexpected, for by June, 1866, both he and. Senator Howe had expressed their belief that the states were required by either the Thirteenth or the Fourteenth Amendment to educate both Negro and white. Both also believed that Congress had the power to prevent the states from making distinctions because of race or color in the administration of their school systems. Sumner felt integration the only satisfactory fulfillment of equality. Howe, on the other hand, did not clearly state his preference for either segregation or integration until 1874, when he said he did not wish legislation to recognize segregation and expressed his belief that Congress could legally require schools to be integrated.

There was one other member of the Thirty-ninth Congress that expressed this same interpretation of the Fourteenth Amendment prior to 1872. In 1870, in discussing a bill to admit Mississippi to representation in Congress, Senator Stewart said the Fourteenth Amendment gave Congress the power to require the states to educate Negroes and whites without discrimination because of race or color. He later said he believed Congress could require integration but stated that he thought it better to leave the states free to decide for themselves how Negroes would be educated.

The consistency in the thought of Sumner, Howe, and Stewart between 1866 and 1874 is in contrast to the inconsistency that marks the comments of other members of the first session of the Thirty-ninth Congress throughout Reconstruction, as already noted, and it is the inconsistency that characterizes the nature of congressional debate with regard to Negro education and civil rights for this entire period.

In 1866 William Lawrence of Ohio interpreted the scope of the civil rights bill to include only those rights enumerated in the bill itself. He also said the states were free to regulate such things as suffrage and the selection of jurors. In 1874, however, he spoke in defense of a civil rights bill that did pertain to the selection of jurors.[1] This altered position is typical of the general Radical shift--its changing interpretation of the scope of civil equality that it sought to guarantee through congressional legislation.

Sherman and Boutwell also shifted ground, although the contrast is not so clear as it is with Lawrence. Sherman and Boutwell defended Sumner's civil rights bill between 1872 and 1875, and both had also referred to education when defending a civil rights bill in 1865. Neither, however, had mentioned education in 1866 or had tried to incorporate reference to education in either the 1866 civil rights bill or the Fourteenth Amendment. It is clear that neither envisioned later civil rights legislation. Sherman, for example, had opposed Sumner's 1867 proposal to make provision for

Negro education by stating it was unnecessary, and. Boutwell said in 1869 that the Fifteenth Amendment was the last reconstruction on measure.

Radicals were consistent, however, in their comments concerning congressional power. in 1866 Robert S. Hale of New York opposed Bingham's February amendment because he considered it a radicals change in the power relationship between state and, federal government. He did vote for the Fourteenth Amendment, however, as though he had become reconciled to this change. Then in 1875 he defended the constitutionality of the civil rights bill by noting his earlier observation with regard to the change in the balance of power between the state and federal government.

It was this change in the power structure that Conservatives attacked in 1866 and, then denied later in 1872.

Michael Kerr of Indiana and Garrett Davis of Kentucky exemplify this Conservative shift. In 1866 Kerr attacked the civil rights bill by saying it encroached upon state power. It would, he said, allow Congress to require Negroes to be educated with whites. In 1871, however, in opposition to an enforcement bill, Kerr denied that Congress had the power to enforce the guarantees of section one of the Fourteenth Amendment. This attack upon congressional power in 1871 was a prelude to the nature of Conservative opposition to Sumner's civil rights bill.

Davis criticized Sumner's bill by saying its provisions were not sanctioned by the Constitution.[2] In 1866, however he had said the civil rights bill would prevent a state from exercising its power to keep Negroes and whites separate in public transportation, hotels, and churches. He had also spoken of Radical efforts at this time as an attempt to "revolutionize" the government.

There is one other shift that is unique. In 1866 Lot M. Morrill of Maine defended Radical efforts and argued with Garrett Davis by noting that civil rights legislation was "revolutionary" because of the results of the war. Then in 1872, in language as "conservative" as that employed by Davis himself, Morrill claimed the Fourteenth Amendment did, not give Congress power to pass Sumner's civil rights bill.

These varied shifts are to be expected when one considers the political struggle between Radical and Conservative elements and the diversity of thought with regard to questions pertaining to education *per se* and the role and status to be assumed by the Negro in society. Those that believed any matter pertaining to education belonged solely within State jurisdiction, and those that shared with Southerners their opinions about the Negro were naturally led to interpret the Constitution in light of these more basic interests. As the Radicals shifted ground, then, so, too, would the more "conservative" position. Radical plans to control Congress, on the other hand, and to elevate the status of the Negro--whether from a political or humanitarian motive--also led them naturally to interpret the Constitution according to their more basic interests.

Several conclusions seem clear, however. In 1866 it does not appear that education was generally assumed to be within the scope of the Fourteenth Amendment's demand for equality. Before 1872 it was usually said that the Negro needed an education simply because of his new freedom and particularly because of his being granted the suffrage. There are a few exceptions to this pattern of thought, however, which are especially significant when considered with Conservative comments in 1866 that foreshadowed later Radical efforts to integrate the schools. Rowe in 1866, Frelinghuysen in 1867, and. Stewart in 1870--all said the states would be required by the Fourteenth Amendment to educate the Negro without distinctions being made because of race or color.

And Sumner had always believed school integration a necessary aspect of requirements for equality before the law.

It is also clear that the later effort to integrate the schools, even though generally not included in Radical plans in 1866, was consistent with a determined and continual Radical effort to grant to the Negro an equality with the white man before the law.

As for the question of school integration itself, it provoked varied comment whenever raised, among both Radicals and Conservatives. Sumner led efforts to integrate the schools when most felt separate schools sufficient. There was no attempt to integrate the schools in the District of Columbia until Sumner sought to do so; neither was there an effort to integrate the nation's schools until Sumner introduced his civil rights bill in 1870. While Sumner's efforts were unsuccessful, however, the attempts by several to gain congressional recognition of the separate but equal doctrine also failed. It was the objection to this doctrine, in fact, that killed all reference to education in the later civil rights bill as finally passed.

In the following chapters it will be seen how the states handled an issue left to them by Congress throughout Reconstruction. Did state officials feel the Fourteenth Amendment affected their plans to educate the Negro?

FOOTNOTES : CHAPTER IV
SUMMARY: CONGRESS: 1866-1875

1. January 6, 1874, Congressional Record, 43 Cong., 1 sess., I, 412.
2. February 1, 1872, Congressional Globe, 42 Cong., 2 sess., I, 763-764.

CHAPTER 5

RATIFICATION OF THE FOURTEENTH AMENDMENT AND THE EDUCATION OF NEGROES, 1866-1875

A s in Congress, comment at the state level upon section one of the Fourteenth Amendment between 1866 and. 1868 usually contained, no words of interpretation of the scope of this guarantee of civil equality. When specific comment was offered upon the Amendment it generally was related either to section two or to the Amendment as a plan of reconstruction. There were references to Negro education within the states at the time the Fourteenth Amendment was considered by them, but these ordinarily were related to the extension of the suffrage. Indeed, the suffrage question was discussed far more than education. A small number between 1866 and 1868 included Negro education within the definition of civil rights. The segregation question was considered by a few state constitutional conventions convened during Reconstruction, and the issue became directly involved with an interpretation of the Fourteenth Amendment in several court cases of the period.

There was not an interest in the guarantee of civil rights in the states throughout Reconstruction, as there was in Congress, and remarks about civil rights usually were either an elaboration of the rights thought to be included in congressional legislation or a criticism of congressional action. There was little introduction of civil rights bills within state legislatures themselves.

An important development within the states in these years was the inclusion of the Negro in law related to education. Particularly was this true, of course, in the South. In the Border states and in some Northern states the Negro was also included in state law for the first time. And in Connecticut and. Louisiana the schools were integrated by law in 1868.

There was more specific comment upon Negro education and upon the Fourteenth Amendment in Massachusetts than in the other New England states. The Springfield Weekly Republican of July 7, 1866, commented: "...now that whites and blacks are to live together in some measure of equality, with similar rights before the law...it is equally important to both races that education should be freely provided for the blacks.... The negro will by and by become a voter, and he cannot properly exercise the right of suffrage in his present ignorant state."[1] The Boston Daily Advertiser published reconstruction speeches by Benjamin P. Butler and Charles Sumner during the campaign of 1866. Butler said there should be "equal personal rights" and "equal protection under the law," but he did not specify particular rights. Sumner's address was the one in which he recommended additional reconstruction legislation designed to give the Negro a homestead, education, and the suffrage.[2] On October 24, 1866, the Advertiser printed the Fourteenth Amendment with the brief comment: Its terms are "easy" and "just."[3]

Governor Alexander H. Bullock recommended the adoption of the Amendment in general comments upon it in his annual message to the Massachusetts legislature. It would, he said, "give... enduring effect to the provisions of the Act, commonly called the Civil Rights Bill.[4] The legislature ratified the Amendment even though a majority of the committee to which the Amendment had been referred recommended that it not be accepted. The majority report from the committee on federal relations expressed the opinion that to ratify the Amendment would be an admission either that the guarantees of section one were not already in the Constitution or that if there, they had been disregarded to the extent that disregard had been sanctioned by law. If the latter were true, noted the report, then there was no security against similar disobedience of additional guarantees. The rights included. in section one, however, were a part of the Constitution, said the report, and were included in the preamble to the Constitution, in section two of Article Four, and in the First, Second, Fifth, Sixth, and Seventh amendments to the Constitution. There was a minority report from the committee that simply recommended ratification without an elaboration upon the meaning of section one.[5]

Unlike his Massachusetts neighbor, Governor James E. English of Connecticut was not in sympathy with the first session of the Thirty-ninth Congress. He denounced the efforts of Congress particularly because southern people had not been represented in debate of legislation that affected them. Perhaps the Amendment was felt to have affected education, however, for on August 1, 1868, the Connecticut legislature passed the following law: "...no person shall be denied admittance to and instruction in any public school in the school district where such person resides, on account of race or color..."[6]

Governor Paul Dillingham of Vermont praised congregational reconstruction,[7] as did Governor Walter Harriman of New Hampshire. Harriman spoke of suffrage and education as "birthrights of the people." "Not for caste, or race, or color, can any man be debarred from the ballot box, and against no child, however lowly or unfortunate, is closed the door of the school-house."[8]

In New York, too, the governor endorsed the work of Congress. Reuben E. Fenton urged the legislature to ratify the Fourteenth Amendment so that there would be "no delay in anchoring these fraternal guarantees in the Federal Constitution."[9] There were a few references to Negro education in the New York press. The October 16, 1866, issue of the New York Times printed a speech that had been made by Henry Ward Beecher in which he spoke of Negro suffrage and. Negro education as two aspects of reconstruction that had yet to be instituted.[10] The New York Evening Post urged the support of freedmen's schools because "an ignorant class is a dangerous class in a republic."[11] The Evening Post also published the resolutions adopted by a Negro convention in Kansas in which it was stated that the exclusion of persons of color "'from an equal enjoyment of the convenience of public institutions'" was "'unfair,'" "'unjust,'" and "'illegal.'" Railroads, stages, barber-shops, hotels, and saloons were mentioned. This definition of equality was a minority opinion regarding the concept of the scope of civil rights in 1866. Another of the resolutions adopted by this convention called for Negro education as a 'need' of an 'oppressed race just emerging from slavery'."[12]

What were considered by others to be Negro rights were enumerated in the New York Times October 1, 1866: the right to sue and be sued, to earn and receive wages, make contracts, hold real estate, conduct meetings and discuss public questions, to bear arms, and to petition for a redress of grievances,[13]

While editorials in the Times and the Evening Post praised congressional action, those of the New York Herald generally did not. Why the necessity for section one of the Fourteenth Amendment, asked the Herald, when the guarantee of civil rights was assured by the civil rights bill? The sole aim of the Amendment was to make the Negro count in American politics; all else was "mere dress to hide the nakedness of the negro provision."[14]

Between June, 1867, and February, 1868, members of a New York constitutional convention discussed proposals to revise the constitution. In these debates there was no suggestion to change the existing practice whereby both integrated and segregated schools were established.[15] The issue was not discussed, in fact, until 1873, when a civil rights bill was passed that forbade discrimination within the school system because of color.[16]

In contrast to New York and Massachusetts, in Michigan and. Minnesota there seems to have been little discussion of the Fourteenth Amendment. In general terms of approval Governor Henry H. Crapo of Michigan and Governor William R. Marshall of Minnesota recommended ratification of the Amendment.[17] In Michigan, in 1867, a convention convened to revise the constitution. There was no discussion of Negro education in these debates.[18] In1869 there was a case in the Michigan courts involving segregation. A suit was brought again t the board of education for Detroit because it had refused to admit a Negro into one of its schools. Integration was upheld by the Michigan supreme court without reference to the Fourteenth Amendment. The decision was based upon a section of a school law of 1867 that stated: "All residents of any district shall have an equal right to attend any school therein: <u>Provided</u>, That this shall not prevent the grading of schools according to the intellectual progress of the pupils, to be taught in separate places when deemed expedient."[19]

In Wisconsin, the Democratic Daily Milwaukee News attacked congressional policies, interpreting Radical efforts as the Democrats in Congress had interpreted them. In one article it quoted a condemnation of the Fourteenth Amendment from the Boston Commercial and then added: 'All laws preventing negro and white marriages, providing for separate schools, oars, church-pews, etc., for blacks, are also thus to be madeunconstitutional.[20] The Republican press, on the other hand, like Republican comments in Congress, did not offer such an interpretation of the Amendment and spoke of section one in general terms of praise because of its guarantee of civil rights.[21] The Wisconsin State Journal also printed various Republican speeches made in defense of the Amendment. Senator Rowe's address in Congress, in which he referred to Negro education when defending the Fourteenth Amendment, was printed in its entirety. A speech by Lyman Trumbull at Evanston, Illinois, August 31, 1866, was reported; the Senator spoke of section one as embodying the aims of the Thirteenth Amendment and the Civil. Rights Act. And the speech by Carpenter in Milwaukee October 4, 1866, was also quoted. This address, which was also given in Madison October 18, contained no specific comment upon the scope of section one of the Fourteenth Amendment.[22]

Governor Lucius Fairchild endorsed the Amendment, and the majority report of the committee on federal relations also recommended its ratification by the legislature.[23] A minority of one from the committee, Gerrit P. Thorn, opposed the Amendment by charging it an upset of the balance of power between federal and state authority. Echoing Democratic opposition in Congress Thorn said: "The first section, in connection with the fifth, will give to the federal government the supervision of all social and domestic relations of the citizen in the state and to subordinate state governments to federal power."

Republican governors from Western states, like Governor Fairchild, recommended the ratification of the Fourteenth Amendment in language that contained, no interpretation of what was thought to be the scope of section one.[25] The inaugural address of Governor Henry H. Haight of California, however, was somewhat more specific than most gubernatorial speeches. He denounced congressional policies in a defense of the state right to regulate matters related to "civil" and "political rights. He particularly opposed giving the ballot to Negroes and Chinese, or allowing them to hold office. "These inferior races have their civil rights," he claimed, and he mentioned the right to sue and be sued in the courts, to "acquire and possess property," to possess "freedom of person," and to "pursue any lawful occuupation."[26]

The Republican press of this area also defended the Fourteenth Amendment with little comment upon what was thought to be the meaning of section one. An editorial in the San Francisco Evening Bulletin of May 1, 1866, was an exception.

It felt the privileges and immunities clause no different than Article Four, section two, of the Constitution. The remaining clauses of section one, said the Bulletin, extended the guarantee of equal rights to "persons," so that no state, "under the pretense of the regulation of labor, the punishment of vagrancy, etc., could deprive anyone of life, liberty, or property without due process of law or deny to anyone the equal protection of the law.[27] The May 14, 1866, issue of the Portland Morning Oregonian contained an article that also spoke more specifically about the civil rights question than most papers. This article was a letter reported to have been written by George H. Pendleton of Ohio to Nathaniel B. Meade of Virginia in which Pendleton spoke of civil rights that belonged to Negroes in Ohio: "He may acquire and hold property, make contracts, sue and be sued, and give testimony in all courts and in all cases. In some parts of the State, public schools for the benefit of colored children are established under the authority of law, and are supported by the property levied on the taxes [sic] of all the people of the State, and appointed pro rata according to the enumeration of white and colored children."[28]

A Negro paper in San Francisco, The Elevator, occasionally included editorial comments about Negro education. In December, 1870, the paper expressed its dislike of "separate or class institutions" and stated that it supported them only when they were "absolutely necessary." A year later the paper attacked separate schools as a violation of the privileges and immunities clause of the Fourteenth Amendment. This was the first such correlation between education and. the Amendment by the paper.[29]

The segregation issue became involved in the California court in 1874. Mary Francis Ward applied for a writ of mandamus through her father to compel Noah F. Flood to allow her to enter the Broadway Grammar School in San Francisco, of which Flood was the principal. The plaintiff referred to the 1866 Civil Rights Act, the Fourteenth Amendment, The People V. The Board of Education of Detroit (18 Michigan Reports, 401), and Clark V. The Board of Directors (24 Iowa Reports, 267).[30] The argument for the defense contained references to Roberts v. Boston (5 Cushing Reports, 198-206), The People V. The Board of Education of Detroit (18 Michigan Reports, 400, 412), and Clark V. The Board of Directors (24 Iowa Reports, 272). Establishment of separate schools was legal under the police power of the state, said the defense; the Fourteenth Amendment related only to privileges and immunities contained in Article Four, section two, of the Constitution.

The chief justice of the California supreme court, William T. Wallace, said the writ could be refused because of the established fact that the pupil involved did not have sufficient training to qualify her admittance to the school. The court would, however, consider her claim that denial to admit her was because of color and was, therefore, a violation of the Fourteenth Amendment. The issue centered in the equal protection of the laws clause, said Wallace, because education was not one of the privileges and immunities pertaining to United States citizenship and because the due process of law clause was irrelevant. The equal protection of the laws clause "did not create any new or substantive legal right." If no schools were established for the education of Negroes then there would be a violation of this clause, the Justice stated, because California law provided for the education of all the children in the state. Negroes would then have to be admitted to white schools. Provision for Negro education in separate schools, however, was no violation of the equal protection of the law; segregation was a legal alternative for integration. In his decision Wallace referred to the argument for the City of Boston in Roberts v. The City of Boston.[31]

In these Northern and Western states that were furthest removed from the center of attention for reconstruction, then, there is a variety of opinion about education and about the Fourteenth Amendment that includes all types of argument heard in Congress before 1872 when discussing either civil rights or Negro education. The majority defense of the Amendment usually contained no words of interpretation about the effect of section one. There were occasional references to either the rights mentioned in the civil rights bill or to rights guaranteed by the Bill of Rights. And the San Francisco <u>Evening Bulletin</u> referred to Article Four, section two, of the Constitution when speaking of the privileges and immunities clause and then stated that the remaining clauses extended the guarantee of equal rights to all persons, rather than restricting it to citizens. Reference to Negro education was both in terms of its need because of the suffrage and in terms of right. Governor Harriman of New Hampshire spoke of education as a 'birthright,' and a letter of George H. Pendleton published in Oregon mentioned education when discussing civil rights guaranteed Negroes in Ohio. Harriman said nothing of segregation, and Pendleton spoke of separate schools with funds distributed *pro rata* according to the number of white and colored children. In Connecticut, integrated schools were required by a law passed August, 1868.

The minority opposition attacked congressional power conferred by the Fourteenth Amendment because they felt it would give Congress authority to legislate in areas belonging exclusively within state jurisdiction. The article in the <u>Daily Milwaukee News</u> specifically mentioned integration of the schools as a result of the ratification of the Amendment.

There were two judicial aspects of the segregation issue in these states--in Michigan, where integration was upheld without reference to the Fourteenth Amendment, and in California, where segregation was felt legal upon consideration of the Amendment.

These various opinions were also expressed in the states situated between the far Northern states and the Border states. The voice of opposition, however, was somewhat more vociferous.

Governor Marcus L. Ward of New Jersey gave his approval of congressional reconstruction in brief comments upon it in his annual message to the New Jersey legislature,[32] and Governor Andrew O. Curtin of Pennsylvania similarly expressed himself in favor with the Fourteenth Amendment.[33] Two Republican papers in Philadelphia explained what they felt to be the meaning of section one of the Amendment: "...the privileges and immunities of citizens of the United States shall be alike in all the States," said The Philadelphia Inquirer

May 1, 1866, and the Public Ledger spoke of section one as embodying the guarantee of rights in Article Four, section two, of the Constitution.[34] On May 31 the Inquirer stated: "By these Reconstruction resolutions it is designed in the first place to recognize all persons born in the United States to be citizens thereof, without distinction of color. But this only gives them the civil rights incident to free persons, as to life, liberty, and the possession of property. It does not touch the question of political rights, which are left for the States to determine." Several months later, during the fall campaign, the Inquirer referred to the "old law," Section Four, article two, and expressed the opinion that the Fourteenth Amendment went further to extend "the shield of law over all persons born in the United States, or naturalized therein." "Everyone" was guaranteed "a right to live, to labor, to save and to be happy."[35]

In September, 1866, a Southern loyalist convention convened in Philadelphia, and a speech by Frederick Douglass was recorded in the Inquirer. He stated that the Negro wanted "'his civil rights'" and. not "'equal social rights,'" and he referred to "'the right [of the Negro] to be protected in his own family.'"[36]

The Inquirer also spoke of Negro education: "The blacks ought to be educated, but would it not be of equal advantage to establish free schools for the benefit of the whites? They are wanted equally as much as schools for the blacks, and until education is universally diffused throughout the South, the people of that section of all colorss [sic] will be under the domination of the educated classes. This was the case during the rebellion. The 'poor whites' were the serfs of the white aristocracy...."[37]

There was no discussion of Negro education between 1872 and 1873 when a constitutional convention considered the revision of the Pennsylvania constitution. State law at the time said Negroes were to be educated in separate schools when there were enough (20) to warrant the construction of a separate school; otherwise, they were to be educated with whites. [38]

The approval given the Fourteenth Amendment by Governor Jacob D. Cox of Ohio revealed a greater understanding of the Amendment than expressed in most gubernatorial messages. "The first [section] was proven necessary long before the war," said Cox, "when it was notorious that any attempt to exercise freedom of discussion in regard to the system which was then hurrying on the rebellion, was not tolerated in the Southern States; and the state laws gave no real protection to immunities of this kind, which are of the very essence of free government." Continuing in language similar to that used by John A. Bingham in Congress, Cox spoke of the power granted to Congress by the Amendment: "The necessity, also, of having somewhere a reserved right to protect the freedom of the slaves whom the war emancipated is too palpable for argument. If these rights are in good faith protected by State laws and State authorities, there will be no need of federal legislation on the subject, and the power will remain in abeyance; but if they are systematically violated, those who violate them will be themselves responsible for all the necessary interference of the central government."[39]

The Democratic press in Ohio assailed that grant of congressional power. "The fifth section [of the Fourteenth Amendment] is the one that is capable of indefinite mischief," said. The <u>Cincinnati Daily Inquirer</u> June 15, 1866.[40] And in Columbus, <u>The Crisis</u> cried that the Amendment overthrew all state constitutions by depriving states of their right to determine citizenship. The Amendment granted citizenship to "Indians, Negroes, Chinese Coolies, and Gypsies and thereby forced "the Caucasian race to an unnatural equality with the lowest and most degraded types of mankind;" the Amendment was "a direct declaration in favor of mongrelism."[41]

These two papers also either contained speeches or referred to addresses made by fellow Democrats in opposition to the Amendment. Allen O. Thurman charged Congress with trying to make itself "supreme" in state affairs, and Hugh J. Jewett, a railroad man active in politics, claimed that section one of the Amendment would allow Negroes to hold office, to be judges and jurors, and "to distribute the school funds."[42] In a speech at Reading, Pennsylvania, George H. Pendleton attacked section one of the Amendment because it did not enumerate the privileges and immunities that it guaranteed. He also implied that he felt the section unnecessary because of Article Four, section two, of the Constitution.[43] Clement L. Vallandigham also denounced the Amendment in a state rights speech during the fall campaign. He spoke also of the Civil Rights Act, by which, he felt, a Negro could demand entrance into a white railroad car and into a white church.

In 1871 a case involving interpretation of the Fourteenth Amendment regarding separate Negro schools was considered by the Ohio supreme court. At this time Negroes were required to be educated in separate schools. William Garnes applied for a writ of mandamus to compel the directors of his school district to allow his children to attend the white school in the district. He claimed there was a denial of the privileges guaranteed by the Fourteenth Amendment because of the color of his children. The defense stated it was not a case of exclusion, but of classification, as in the grouping by age, sex, and scholarship. There was, therefore, no denial of privileges or immunities or the equal protection of the laws. In a decision containing an argument later used in Congress by those opposed to Sumner's civil rights bill Judge Luther Day declared that school privileges were derived solely from state law, while the Fourteenth Amendment was concerned with privileges and immunities recognized by the Constitution. The rights of Negroes were not abridged in this case, said Day, because there were "equal common school advantages" for Negroes. "Equality of rights does not involve the necessity of educating white and colored persons in the same school, any more than it does that of educating children of both sexes in the same school. Any classification which preserves substantially equal school advantages is not prohibited by either State or federal constitution, nor would, it contravene the provisions of either. There is, then, no ground upon which the plaintiff can claim that his rights under the fourteenth amendment have been infringed."[45]

In Indiana, in 1874, there was also a state supreme court case involving the constitutionality of separate Negro schools. Mary and Edward Carter were denied entrance to a white school in their school district. Their father sought a court order to secure their admission. The school involved objected, but the court overruled the demurrer, and this decision favorable to Carter was upheld in the Marion Superior Court upon appeal. The supreme court reversed the judgment of the superior court, however, and stated that separate schools were no violation of the terms of the Fourteenth Amendment. School privileges were not included within the "fundamental rights" enumerated in Corfield V. Coryall, said Chief Justice Samuel H. Buskirk, nor were school rights covered by the scope of the Thirteenth Amendment and the 1866 Civil Rights Act. The privileges and immunities clause of the Fourteenth Amendment, said the Chief Justice, related only to the privileges and immunities belonging to United States citizenship, as declared in the Slaughter House decision. In discussing the equal protection of the laws clause Buskirk referred to The State v. Gibson (36 Indiana Reports, 389), a case in 1871 that involved the intermarriage of white and Negro. The court had declared then that the Fourteenth Amendment extended the "blessings of the Constitution and laws to a new class of persons" but did not grant power to Congress to regulate the "domestic institutions of a state." At that time, noted Buskirk, there was no judicial precedent for an interpretation of the Fourteenth Amendment; now, however, that decision of 1871 was upheld by the Ohio decision, Garnes v. McCann. Education, said the Chief Justice, was "purely a domestic institution, and the state had the power to make classifications that would "concern the good order and success of the system." Buskirk noted that the same session of Congress that framed the Fourteenth Amendment believed that it was not prevented from establishing separate Negro Schools in the District of Columbia, and no session had felt differently since then, he concluded.[46]

Oliver P. Norton had been governor of Indiana when the Fourteenth Amendment was first considered by the Indiana legislature. At that time he expressed general favor with Reconstruction legislation. He also recommended that Negroes be included in the Indiana school law, but he felt they should be educated separate from the whites. Thomas A. Hendricks was the governor of Indiana between 1872 and 1876. As a member of the first session of the Thirty-ninth Congress he had been unopposed to the Civil Rights Act, but had voted against the Fourteenth Amendment. During his governorship he did not question the school segregation that had been established within the state by law in 1869.[47]

There was one other case involving segregation in this reconstruction period, and the decision came just a few months before the ratification of the Fourteenth Amendment. Through her father's application for a writ of mandamus, Susan B. Clark of Muscatine, Iowa, sought admission to a white school. The case involved interpretation of Iowa law declaring that an education be given all children without distinction of color. The school board maintained there was authority to separate the schools because of discretionary powers granted the board by the state. In a decision similar to that of the Michigan court in 1869 Judge Chester C. Cole maintained that the board's discretionary power could not be exercised to make distinctions founded upon color. Separate schools could not be established for Irish children, German children, or African children, said Cole. "In other words, all the youths are equal before the law" and there is no power vested in the school board to "disturb that equality."[48]

During that same year the governor of Iowa recommended ratification of the Fourteenth Amendment by the Iowa legislature. His remarks contain no interpretation of the Amendment, however.[49] Similar general comments were made by the governor of Illinois, Richard J. Ogleby, in 1867.[50] A Republican press in Illinois also gave little indication of what it thought the meaning of section one of the Amendment to be.

The Chicago Tribune, however, did refer to the right to bring suit in a court and the right to purchase, hold, sell, and inherit property when speaking of the scope of the Amendment's guarantee of rights.[51] There was also a reference to Negro education in the Tribune. If Southerners did not educate the Negro, said the paper, then others would; education followed the granting of the suffrage.[52]

Between 1869 and 1870 a constitutional convention, convened to revise the Illinois constitution, and in the discussions of this convention there was no reference to Negro education. Illinois school law at this time said nothing of the Negro. There was a gradual acceptance of the idea that Negroes were included within its scope, however, and separate schools were established for them, although occasionally schools were integrated. This interpretation of the law culminated in 1874, when the legislature passed a bill "to protect colored children in their rights to attend public schools."[53]

Both the governors of Nebraska and Kansas recommended that their legislatures ratify the Fourteenth Amendment in general, undefined terms.[54] In Kansas, the <u>Atchison Daily Champion</u> was among the few Republican voices in 1866 that referred to education as a civil right within the scope of the Fourteenth Amendment. The <u>Champion</u> enumerated, the following Negro rights: "to enter schools and receive the advantages of education," to labor and enjoy the results of toil, "to build churches and worship God," to acquire and, hold property, and to obtain redress of injuries in the courts. There was no specific comment upon segregation, however. In another editorial listing the some rights the <u>Champion</u> spoke of the Negro right "to erect schools and receive education," again with no word about segregation.

In 1874 the Kansas legislature passed a civil rights bill that forbade discrimination because of color in the public schools, hotels, inns, boarding houses, places of entertainment requiring a state license, steamboats, railroads, stagecoaches, omnibuses, streetcars, and any other means of transportation.[56] It is not clear whether this bill was meant to integrate the schools. It was worded: "...if any of the regents or trustees of any state university, college, or other school of public instruction, or the state superintendent... make any distinction on account of race, color or previous condition of servitude, the person so offending shall be deemed guilty of a misdemeanor." While this seems to indicate integration, Negroes evidently continued to be educated in separate schools in some areas.[57]

Kansas was one of few states that concerned itself with civil rights legislation and one of few states during the period 1866-1868 in which there was reference to education as a civil right. The inclusion of education by the <u>Atchison Daily Champion</u> when enumerating rights guaranteed by the Fourteenth Amendment was a minority interpretation of the scope of the Amendment by those favorable to it at the state level. The <u>Champion</u> did not refer to the segregation issue, however. With the possible exception of some Southern Radical opinion, when the Fourteenth Amendment was considered by the states only the Democratic opposition expressed the opinion that the Amendment might require integration in the schools and other public institutions. In these states just north and west of the Border states, for example, Clement C. Vallandigham attacked the Amendment because he felt it would give Congress the power to integrate railroads and. churches. Other comments about education in these states were not related to the civil rights issue. The <u>Philadelphia Inquirer,</u> for example, felt Southern and "poor white education necessary in order to keep them from the control of the white aristocracy."

In addition to the <u>Atchison</u> opinion about Negro education, there were two other comments upon the Amendment in this area that were more significant than most references to the Amendment. The <u>Philadelphia Inquirer</u> spoke of section one as a measure extending the guarantee of constitutional rights to all persons, rather than just to citizens. And Governor Cox of Ohio felt the congressional power granted by the Amendment would be used only if the states failed to secure all persons in their rights and privileges.

Of the three court cases in this area two upheld segregation upon a consideration of the Fourteenth Amendment and one sustained integration before the Amendment was ratified by the states. This latter decision, however, did speak of integration as a requirement of the concept, equality before the law.

In the remaining states the majority opinion of the Amendment in 1866 was one of condemnation of what was felt to be the overthrow of state authority to legislate in the field of civil rights. Radical governments in the South changed the nature of official comment upon the Amendment, of course, and opinions expressed under these regimes reflect the more general approval given the Amendment by other Republicans.

The [Baltimore] <u>Sun</u> attacked the Fourteenth Amendment, with particular reference to section two, and Governor Thomas Swann of Maryland felt that section five would leave the Southern and Border states "at the mercy of the majority in Congress, in all future time." He also particularly criticized Negro suffrage.[58] A report from the joint committee on federal relations recommended that the Amendment not be ratified by the legislature because it conferred power upon Congress to legislate in areas reserved for state authority and because questions of citizenship and civil rights were already settled by the Constitution.[59]

There was no comment upon Negro education in Maryland in 1867, when a convention met to revise the state constitution. At this time Negroes were not included in the school law, but beginning April, 1868, separate schools were to be established for them.[60]

In West Virginia Negroes were also required to be educated in separate schools, and this provision was written into the revised constitution of 1872.[61]

In Kentucky, Governor Thomas E. Bramlette objected to the Amendment because it had not been submitted to the states in accordance with the requirements of the Constitution, and in Missouri Governor Thomas C. Fletcher gave his approval of the Amendment with only brief comment upon St.[62] A "Petition of Colored Citizens" sent to the Missouri legislature in 1865 asked that schools be constructed for them and that the elective franchise be extended to them. "We would enter, at once," said the petition, "upon the work of our education, so as to be prepared to meet intelligently and skillfully all the responsibilities and duties of enfranchised manhood." Separate Negro schools were required by law in Missouri throughout Reconstruction, while in Kentucky, in 1869, a law recognizing the establishment of separate Negro schools, which had been passed in 1867 was repealed.[63]

In Arkansas, Governor Isaac Murphy recommended the ratification of the Fourteenth Amendment, and his reason for doing so was different than any other explanation given at this time for the necessity of ratification: "An extensive railroad system is ready to start into rapid construction as soon as the political condition of the State renders it safe in the judgment of capitalists.... The ratification or rejection of this amendment, by the present legislature, requires serious, calm, and unprejudiced deliberation. In settling this great reconstruction question, statesmen will be influenced only by the general good or bad results that are likely to follow from their decision. What effect will that decision have on the railroad interests of the State, on our prospective manufacturing interests, and on our commercial and agricultural interests? What effect will it have in allaying or increasing sectional contention; and how will it, in fine, affect the general peace, prosperity, and good order of society in all its classifications."[64] Feeling other "interests" more important, the Arkansas legislature approved 68-2 a resolution from the committee on federal relations advising rejection of the Amendment.[65] The report from the committee was a denunciation of Radical efforts.[66]

In April, 1868, Governor Murphy again recommended ratification of the Amendment, and. a Radical legislature approved his recommendation. This time the Governor's message simply stated that ratification was necessary if Arkansas were to be recognized as a state in the Union.[67] In January and February of that year a Radical constitution had been framed, and in discussing this constitution there was no debate on Negro education. The article on education contained no comment about color or race. During the roll call for the vote of adoption of the constitution there were occasional criticisms of the section on education--that either Negroes should not be educated or should not be educated with whites. There was no reference to the Fourteenth Amendment. On July 23, 1868, a school law was passed that required schools to be segregated.[68]

In contrast to Arkansas and the other Southern states, Tennessee was able to ratify the Fourteenth Amendment in 1866 because her government had been "reconstructed by that time. In his brief comments to the special session of the legislature in July, 1866, Governor William G. Brownlow referred to section one of the Amendment as simply the guarantee to all citizens of "equal protection in the enjoyment of life, liberty and property." Minority reports from both houses, however, felt there was more to the Amendment than conceded by the Republicans. The house report stated the Amendment removed all distinctions of race, and the senate report assailed the attack upon state rights and unsuccessfully moved to add a proviso to the resolution of ratification that the Amendment would not be construed either to give Negroes the suffrage or to allow them to hold, office, sit on juries, or marry white persons.[69]

In 1870 Tennessee revised her constitution, inserting a requirement that schools be segregated. This provision was added to the report on education as it came from committee and was approved 72-1. School segregation had been required by state law since March 5, 1867. Prior to that time there had been no provision made for Negro education.[70]

Unlike most conservative Southern governors, Francis H. Pierpont of Virginia recommended the ratification of the Fourteenth Amendment because, he said, as a reconstruction measure its terms were not so hard as they might have been.[71] The governors of North and South Carolina, on the other hand, attacked the Amendment as a measure giving power to Congress to regulate state affairs. Jonathan Worth of North Carolina spoke of section five as "mischievous and dangerous," and James L. Orr of South Carolina particularly condemned federal authority to legislate in matters related to citizenship and suffrage.[72]

Virginia schools were organized on the basis of segregation; those in the Carolinas, however, were not. In the Radical constitutional convention of North Carolina there was some discussion of the question of separate Negro schools, however Albion W. Tourgee moved to amend a proposal requiring segregation by stating that separate schools could be established so long as they were equal to the schools for whites. Both his substitute and the original motion were defeated, and the section on education simply referred to the education of all the children of the state. Schools were required to be segregated, however, by law passed March 1, 1873.[73]

The article on education that was incorporated, into the South Carolina constitution read: "All the public schools, colleges, and universities of this State, supported in whole or in part by the public funds, shall be free and open to all the children and youth of the State, without regard to race or color." This was felt by some to require integration, but Negroes were generally educated in separate schools during Reconstruction.[74] In the Radical constitutional convention for South Carolina there had been a discussion of integration without reference to the Fourteenth Amendment, although Francis L. Cardoso spoke of the section on education as a part of reconstruction legislation that secured political and civil equality. He also felt schools could be segregated under this section.[75]

There was also some consideration of segregation in the Georgia Radical constitutional convention of 1868. As reported from committee the article on education provided for the voluntary establishment of separate departments and schools for such scholars as may be required, with the condition that there be no partiality" in the separation. This aspect of the section on education was dropped, however, and it was worded with no reference to the segregation issue.[76]

In 1866 Governor Charles J. Jenkins of Georgia had focused his criticism of the Fourteenth Amendment upon section two. It was recorded in The [Milledgeville] Southern Recorder that he also had opposed section one because it took "discretionary power from the ate tea in matters related to civil rights, The committee in the Georgia legislature that had considered the Fourteenth Amendment in 1866 recommended its rejection. It offered no interpretation of the Amendment, but criticized Congress for framing it without the representation of Georgia, who was considered to be a state in the Union only for the purpose of ratification.[77] In 1868 Governor Rufus B. Bullock advised the Radical legislature to ratify the Amendment; his comments were brief and general.[78]

There was one reference to Negro education in Southern Recorder at the time the Fourteenth Amendment was considered by Congress and by Georgia in 1866. The Negro needed education now that he was the master of his destiny, said the Recorder, and it was better that the South educate him than for the North to do it.[79]

Like Jenkins of Georgia, the Democratic governors of Florida, Mississippi, and Texas attacked the Fourteenth Amend- sent as a measure radically altering the relationship between state and federal authority, and reports from the committees on federal relations in Mississippi and Texas contained familiar words of condemnation.[80] In July, 1870, the Radical Mississippi legislature passed a bill protecting citizens in their right to travel upon all public conveyances in the state in April, 1873, the Radical Texas legislature passed a law requiring schools to be segregated. Since 1867 there had been no specific reference to the Negro in Texas school law.[81]

Louisiana was unique among the Radical states of the South because of its policy to integrate the schools. In most Southern states neither segregation nor integration was recognized by Radical law, although in practice nearly all schools were segregated. Whether the Fourteenth Amendment was felt to have required integration by the Radical government in Louisiana is not certain.

A report from the committee on federal relations in 1866 said that in Louisiana "free persons of color" had long possessed the right to acquire education, to testify in courts of justice, to hold property, and to be protected in person and. property. This report evidently concerned the Fourteenth Amendment, which the committee felt unnecessary.[82] The only other reference to the Amendment in 1866 was an editorial in The Daily Picayune October 2, when it was said that section one was simply a restatement of the principle of equality expressed in the Civil Rights Act.[83]

In 1866 the Negro press in New Orleans spoke of education without any reference to either the Civil Rights Act or the Fourteenth Amendment.[84] In 1867 however, the paper spoke of integrated schools as a requirement of the concept, equality before the law. Separate schools, said the New Orleans Tribune, was "inequality before the law," because the act of separation itself caused a "distinction to be made that was not equality. Authority to integrate the schools, said the Tribune, was granted by the Civil Rights Act.[85]

In 1868 the Radical constitution was framed in language that required integrated education: "There shall be no separate schools or institutions of learning established exclusively for any race by the State of Louisiana." On September 25, 1868, Governor Henry C. Warmouth vetoed a civil rights bill because, he said, the rights therein enumerated were already guaranteed by the State constitution. The bill sought the destruction of discrimination made because of color in public conveyances, places of public resort, businesses requiring a state license, and in water and rail transportation.[86]

In 1870 the Negro paper, The Louisianian, recorded the Republican platform adopted at the state convention for that year. Included in this platform was the declaration that the party supported "the principles of equal rights to all mankind, whether at the ballot box, in the public schools, or in the pursuit of business.[87]

The scope given the concept of equal rights was certainly broader in Louisiana than in most other states. Only in some

Northern states were schools also integrated by law: Massachusetts, Connecticut, Michigan (by court interpretation), and Iowa (by court interpretation). In Kansas there was expression given to the concept of equality before the law by those favorable to reconstruction measures that was also more comprehensive than in most states. Unlike Louisiana, however, the schools in Kansas were not required to be integrated, and the settlement of the segregation issue was left to the discretion of each school district. In South Carolina, Francis L. Cardozo felt schools could be segregated, but he also referred to education as a part of reconstruction legislation securing political and civil equality. The <u>Wisconsin State Journal</u> printed the congressional speech of Senator Howe in which he referred to Negro education when defending the Fourteenth Amendment, and the <u>Morning Oregonian</u> printed a letter written by George H. Pendleton in which he spoke of Negro education when discussing civil rights guaranteed Negroes in Ohio. Rowe had, not expressed his opinion about the segregation question, and, Pendleton had spoken of separate schools for Negroes.

As in Congress, however, most of those defending the Fourteenth Amendment at the state level either did not explain their ideas of the scope of section one or did not refer to education when speaking of particular rights that would be guaranteed by it. When there was comment upon the scope of section one it usually included reference either to the rights enumerated in the Civil Rights Act or to rights guaranteed by the Bill of Rights, and when there was reference to Negro education it generally was related to the extension of the suffrage.

Other references to education at the time the Fourteenth Amendment was considered by the states were expressed by the Democratic opposition. The <u>Daily Milwaukee News</u> stated that integrated schools would be required if the Amendment became law, and the minority report from the Wisconsin legislative committee on federal relations also expressed this type of concern when it condemned the Amendment as a measure giving Congress power to regulate the "social and domestic relations' of a state. Similarly, Clement C. Vallandigham attacked the Amendment because he felt it would require the integration of railroads and churches.

As with most of those favoring the ratification of the Fourteenth Amendment, however, most of those opposed to it did not state their opinions regarding the scope of section one. The majority of the opposition merely attacked the change in the relationship between state and federal power.

Finally, the court cases involving segregation are to be noted. In three state supreme court cases of this period separate schools were upheld upon a consideration of the Fourteenth Amendment. In two cases integration was sustained without reference to the Fourteenth Amendment, although both involved interpretation of the expression of equal rights in state law.

Except for these court decisions, in none of the changes or interpretations of school law affecting Negro education during this period was it recorded that the Fourteenth Amendment was considered to have been related to those changes. One receives the impression that the passage of the Fourteenth Amendment and the inclusion of the Negro in state school law for the first time generally were events independent of one another. They resulted from the same cause--the need to hide the nakedness of emancipation--rather than standing themselves in the relationship of cause and effect.

In these states making initial provision for Negro education, except for Louisiana, schools were generally segregated, which suggests either that the Fourteenth Amendment was not felt to require integration or that it was not thought to have any relation to the issue. In the states that had provided for Negro education prior to 1866, except for Connecticut, no change occurred in school policy during Reconstruction, which again suggests either that the Fourteenth Amendment was felt to be compatible with existing practice--everything from required segregation to required inte-gration--or that it was thought not to have any bearing upon the question.

That some felt the Fourteenth Amendment affected education, however, is evident because of the existence of thought at the time that referred to Negro education when discussing the Fourteenth Amendment. And such isolated cases as the school integration re-quired in Connecticut and Louisiana in 1868 seem particularly to be related to the Amendment's demand for equality before the law, although it cannot be said conclusively that the Amendment brought about this integration.

If the Fourteenth Amendment were generally felt to have been related to the education of Negroes then this belief would most likely be reflected within the state departments of education. It is the purpose of the following and concluding chapter to ascertain the degree to which the Fourteenth Amendment was thought to be related to education by those responsible for it.

FOOTNOTES: CHAPTER V

Ratification of the Fourteenth Amendment and the Education of Negroes

1. Springfield Weekly Republican, July 7, 1866, 2.
2. Boston Daily Advertiser, September 1, 1866, 1; October 3 1866, 1. Supra, III, 81.
3. Ibid., October 24, 1866, 1.4.
4. Alexander H. Bullock, Governor's Message, January 4, 1867, Documents printed by Order of the Senate of the Commonwealth of Massachusetts During the Session of the General Court, A.D. 1867 (Boston: Wright and Potter, 1867), doc. no. 1, pp. 68-69.
5. Documents Printed by Order of the House of Representatives of the Commonwealth of Massachusetts During The Session of the General Court, A.D. 1867 (Boston: Wright and Potter, 1867), doc. no. 149, pp. 2-4, 25. The schools in Massachusetts had been integrated since 1855.
6. James E. English, Governor's Message, May 1, 1867, Public Documents of the Legislature of Connecticut, May Session, 1867 (Hartford: Case, Lockwood and Company, 1867), doc. no. 2, p. 6.
7. Paul Dillingham, Governor's Message, October 12, 1866, Vermont Legislative Documents and Official Reports, Annual Session of the General Assembly, 1866 (Montpelier, 1866), doc. no 1, p. 26.
8. Walter Harriman, Governor's Message, June 6, 1867, <u>Journal of the House of Representatives of the State of New Hampshire</u> (Manchester: John B. Clarke, 1867), "Appendix," 609.
9. Reuben E. Fenton, Governor's Message, January 2, 1867, <u>Documents of the Assembly of the State of New York. Ninetieth</u>

Session--1867 (Albany: C. Van Benthuuysen and. Sons, 1867), I, doc. no. 2, p. 2.

10. New Fork Times, October, 16, 1866, 1.
11. New York Evening Post, October 19, 1866, 1.
12. New York Evening Post, October 30, 1866, 2. No reference to this convention was found in the Kansas press examined (Atchison Daily Champion).
13. New York Times, October 1 1866, 4.
14. New York Herald, May 3, 1866; May 31, 1866, 4.
15. Journal of the Convention of the State of New York (Albany: Weed, Parsons and Company, 1867). Proceedings and Debates of the Constitutional Convention of the State of New York, (Albany: Weed, Parsons and Company, 1868).

    Ira Harris, who had been a member of the Joint Committee of Fifteen, was a member of this constitutional convention.
16. Journal of the Assembly of the State of New York: at their Ninety-Sixth Session (Albany: The Argus Company, 1813), 1, 615-616. Journal of the Senate of the State of New York: at Their Ninety-Sixth Session (Albany: The Argus Company, 1873), 507.

    Albert Blum,"Summary of States Reports" (MSS of material examined for the NAACP in the case of Brown v. Topeka), 2. This "Summary" indicates state legislation regarding Negro education during Reconstruction. Blum indicates that this bill forbade school directors to discriminate because of color. Whether it required schools to be integrated is not certain; it probably did not.
17. Henry H. Crapo, Governor's Message, January 2, 1867, Joint Documents of the State of Michigan for the Year 1866 (Lansing: John A. Kerr, 1866), doc. no. 1, p. 47. William Marshall, Governor's Message, January 10, 1867, Executive Documents of the State of Minnesota for the Year 1866 (St. Paul: Press Printing Co., 1868), doc. no. , p. 26.

18. Journal of the Constitutional Convention of the State of Michigan (Lana: John A. Kerr and Co., 1867). Debates and Proceedings of the Constitutional Convention of the State of Michigan (Lansing: John A. Kerr and Co., 1867).

19. The People ex rel. Joseph Workman v. The Board of Education of Detroit (18 Michigan Reports, 400). The argument for the school, board centered in the contention that segregation did not constitute exclusion, but regulation of the system resulting from legal discretionary power. The court maintained that discretionary power was subject to general regulations, such as the section of law involved. Judge James V. Campbell dissented, upholding the argument of the school board.

    Negroes had been included in the Michigan school law prior to 1867. There had probably been both segregated and integrated schools up until 1869 (Infra., V, is?).

20. Daily Milwaukee News, June 19, 1866, 4. It is not clear whether this interpretation was a paraphrasing of the Commercial article or the opinion of the News.

21. Wisconsin State Journal, May 1, 1866, 1.

22. Ibid. June 18 19, 20, 1866, 2; September 5, 1866, 2; October a8 1866, October 19 1866, 2.

23. Lucius Fairchild, Governor's Message, January 10, 1867, Governor's Message and Accompanying Documents for the State of Wisconsin, for the Year A.D. 1867 (Madison: Atwood and Rublee, 1867) doc. no. 1, xxii-xxiv.

24. Journal of the Senate of Wisconsin, for the Year A.D. 1867 (Madison: Atwood. and Rublee, 1867), 7-93.

25. H.G. Blasdel, Governor's Message, January 10, 1867, Journal of the Senate During the Third Session of the State of Nevada (Carson City: Joseph E. Eckley, 1867), "Appendix," doc. "B," 9-10. Negroes were required to be educated in separate schools (Infra, V, 158).

George L. Woods, Governor's Message, September 12, 1866, <u>Journal of the Proceedings of th House of the Legislative Assembly of Oregon, for the Fourth Regular Session, 1866</u> (Salem: W.A. McPherson, 1866), 26-30.

Frederick F. Low, Governor's Message, December 2, 1867, <u>The Journal of the Assembly During the Seventeenth Session of the Legislature of the State of California, 1867-8</u> (Sacramento: D.W. Gelwicks, 1868), 53-54.

26. Henry B. Haight, Governor's Message, December 5, 1867, <u>The Journal of the Assembly During the Seventeenth Session of the Legislature of the State of California</u>, 99-100.
27. San Francisco <u>Evening Bulletin</u>, May 1, 1866, 2.
28. George H. Pendleton to Nathaniel B. Meade, December 21, 1865, Portland <u>Morning Oregonian</u>, May 14, 1866, 1.
29. <u>The Elevator</u>, December 2, 1870, 2; December 29, 1871, 2. Only scattered issues of <u>The Elevator</u> are available, so there may have been an earlier reference to the Fourteenth Amendment. There seems to have been no questioning of the constitutionality of separate schools prior to 1871, however, Articles related to Negro schools through 1869 and 1870 contain no reference either to the Amendment or to civil rights.
30. The Iowa decision of April, 1868, upheld integration upon the consideration of state law (Infra, 134).
31. Ward V. Flood (<u>The California Reports</u>, 36). Since 183 Negroes had been required to be educated in separate schools (<u>Infra</u>, V, 159).
32. Marcus L. Ward, Governor's Message, January 18, 1867, <u>Documents of the Ninety-First Legislature of the State of New Jersey</u> (New Brunswick: J.P. Babcock, 1867), doc. no. 1, p. 26.
33. Andrew G. Curtin to Colonel Fr. Jordan, <u>The Philadelphia Inquirer</u>, July 13, 1866, 4. Jordan was chairman of the Union State Central Committee centered in Philadelphia. This correspondence recorded in the <u>Inquirer</u> was related to Curtin's

unsuccessful attempt to get other governors to call extra legislative sessions to ratify the Fourteenth Amendment.

34. The Philadelphia Inquirer, May 1, 1866, 4; The Philadelphia Public Ledger, September 27, 1866, 2.

35. The Philadelphia Inquirer, May 31, 1866, 4; October 1 1866, 4.

36. The Philadelphia Inquirer, September 7, 1866, 3.

37. Ibid., September 11, 1866, 4.

38. Journal of the Convention to Amend the Constitution of Pennsylvania (Harrisburg: Benjamin Singerly, 1873). Debates of the Convention to Amend the Constitution of Pennsylvania (Harrisburg: Benjamin Singerly, 1873), I, 676-677.

    Sixteenth Report of the Superintendent of Public Instruction for the State of Indiana (Indianapolis: Alexander H. Conner, 1869), 25. (This records a letter from the Pennsylvania superintendent of education to the Indiana superintendent. Infra, V, 161.)

39. Jacob D. Cox, Governor's Message, January 2, 1867, Message and Annual Reports for 1866, Made to the Fifty-Seventh General Assembly, of the State of Ohio (Columbus: L.D. Myers and Bro., 1867), I, doc, no. 18, p 282.

40. The Cincinnati Daily Inquirer, June 15, 1866, 2.

41. The Crisis, June 27, 1866, 169.

42. The Cincinnati Daily Inquirer, May 25, 1866; 2; The Crisis, July 4, 1866, 178.

43. The Crisis, August 1, 1866, 210.

44. Ibid., October 24, 1866, 307.

45. The State of Ohio, ex rel. William Garnes v. John W. McCann, and Others (21 Ohio Reports, 198). In 1873 Negroes were allowed by law to be educated with whites if there were no objections raised within the school district affected (Infra, V, 163). Apparently this change in law proceeded from the need to legalize the practice whereby in some areas Negroes were allowed to enter white schools.

46. Cory et al. V. Carter (48 Indiana Reports, 327). A petition of Negroes protesting this decision was presented to Congress through Oliver P. Morton, who introduced a resolution "to provide for a writ of error from the supreme court of Indiana to the Supreme Court of the United States in a certain case involving the right of colored citizens." The resolution was referred to the Committee on the Judiciary, where it died. (December 14, 1874, Congressional Record, 43 Cong., 2 sess., I, 65-66. George P. Edmunds, Roscoe Conkling, Matthew H. Carpenter, Frederick J. Frelinghuysen, and Allen G. Thurman were members of this committee.)

47. Oliver P. Morton, Governor's Message, January 11, 1867, Documents of the General Assembly of Indiana at the Forty-Fifth Regular Session (Indianapolis: Samuel M. Douglass, 1867), I, doc. no. 1, p. 21.

    In practice, "by common consent," Negroes were admitted to white schools (Infra, V, 165).

48. Clark v. The Board of Directors (24, Iowa Reports, 266). Judge George G. Wright dissented and stated that the Board could establish separate schools and still maintain an equality before the law between Negro and white. "There is no absolute legal right in a colored child to attend a white school," he said.

49. William M. Stone, Governor's Message, January 14, 1868, Legislative Documents Submitted to the Twelfth General Assembly of the State of Iowa (Des Moines: F.W. Palmer, 1868), I, 28.

50. Richard J. Oglesby, Governor's Message, January 7, 1867, Reports Made to the General Assembly of Illinois, at Its Twenty-Fifth Session, Convened January 7, 1867 (Springfield: Baker, Bailhache and Co., 1867), I, 29.

51. Chicago Tribune, October 10, 1866, 2.

52. Ibid., July 31, 1866, 2.

Journal of the Constitutional Convention of the State of Illinois (Springfield, 1870). Debates and Proceedings of the Constitutional Convention of the State of Illinois (Springfield: Merritt and Brothers, 1870).

53. Journal of the Senate of the Twenty-Eighth General Assembly of the State of Illinois (Springfield, 1874), 528.

54. David Butler, Governor's Message, May 17, 1867, Senate Journal of the State Legislature of Nebraska (Omaha: St. A.D. Balcombe, 1867), 57-58. S.J. Crawford, Governor's Message, January 8, 1867, Senate Journal of the State of Kansas (Leavenworth: Clarke, Emery and. Co., 1867), 143-45.

55. Atchison Daily Champion, June 3, 1866, 2; June 29, 1866, 2.

56. The Laws of the State of Kansas passed at the Fourteenth Annual Session of the Legislature (Topeka: Geo. W. Martin, 1874), 82-83.

57. Segregation had been an issue within the state department of education throughout Reconstruction. Undoubtedly there would have been strong negative reaction to this bill if it were felt to require integration. As it was, however, there was no reference to the bill in the annual reports of the county and state superintendents of education (Infra, V, 173;).

58. The Sun, April 30, 1866, 2; May 4, 1866, 2.

Thomas Swann, Governor's Message, January 4, 1867, Journal of the Proceedings of the Senate of Maryland, January Session, 1867 (Annapolis: Henry A.Lucas, 1867), doc. "A," 25.

59. Ibid., doc. "I," 13-14. George Vickers, who was later a United States senator that opposed Sumner's civil rights bill, was a member of this committee.

60. Proceedings of the State Convention of Maryland to Frame a New Constitution (Anapolis: George Colton, 1867). It was also provided at this time that Negroes could testify in court (Ibid., 148-150).

Public Documents of the House of Delegates of Maryland, January Session, 1868 (Anapolis: Wm. Thompson of R., 1868), doc. "X."

61. Journal of the Constitutional Convention (Charleston: Henry S. Walker, 1872). West Virginia was one of four states that wrote segregation into a constitution revised during Reconstruction. The other three ere Texas (1866), Tennessee (1870), and Missouri (1865, 1875). Radical constitutions generally did not require either integration or segregation. The Louisiana constitution required schools to be integrated, and in South Carolina there was concern that the constitution might be interpreted to require them. Constitutions revised in other states during this period--Illinois, Maryland, Nebraska, and Pennsylvania--contained general education provisions that did not specifically refer to the Negro.

62. Thomas E. Bramlette, Governor's Message, January 4, 1867, Journal of the Senate of the Commonwealth of Kentucky (Frankfort: John H. Harvey, 1867), 17-21. Thomas C. Fletcher, Governor's Message, January 4, 1867, Journal of the Missouri State Senate (Jefferson City: Emory S. Foster, 1867), 14-15.

63. Appendix to the Senate Journal of the Adjourned Session of the Twenty Third General Assembly of the State of Missouri (Jefferson City: Emory S. Foster, 1865-6), 570.

"Annual Report of the Superintendent of Public Instruction, Kentucky Documents 1871. (no title page), II, 99- 100.

64. Isaac Murphy, Governor's Message, November 8, 1866, Journal of the Senate of Arkansas (Little Rock: Price and Barton, 1870), 51.

65. Journal of the House of Representatives (Little Rock: Price and Barton, 1870), 291.

66. Ibid., 285-289.

67. Isaac Murphy, Governor's Message, April 3, 1868, Journal of the Senate of Arkansas (Little Rock: Price and Barton, 1869), 18-19.

68. Debates and Proceedings of the Convention Which Assembled at Little Rock, January 7, 1868 (Little Rock: J.G. Price, 1868), 660, 672, 673.

   Journal of the Senate of Arkansas (Little Rock: Price and Barton, 1869), 239. Journal of the Assembly of the State of Arkansas at Their Seventeenth Session (Little Rock: John G. Price, 1868, 1870), I, 257. A few senators objected to the requirement for segregation, saying it was contrary to a republican form of government. They felt the matter should be left to the discretion of each school district (Journal of the Senate..., 239).

69. House Journal of the Called Session of the General Assembly of the State of Tennessee (Nashville: S.C. Mercer, 1866), 26-27, 37-38. Senate Journal of the Called Session of the General Assembly of the State of Tennessee (Nashville: S.C. Mercer, 1866), 41-42.

70. Journal of the Proceedings of the Convention of Delegates Elected by the People of Tennessee to Amend, Revise, or Form and Make a New Constitution for the State (Nashville: Jones, Purvis and Co., 1870), 307-30S, 309.

   First Report of the Superintendent of Public Instruction (Nashville: Edgar Grisham, 1859), 5, 17.

71. Francis H. Pierpont, Governor's Message, December 4, 1866, Journal of the Senate of the Commonwealth of Virginia (Richmond: James E. Goode, 1866), 28-34.

72. Jonathan Worth, Governor's Message to the Legislature of 1866-1867, Executive and Legislative Documents Laid Before the General Assembly of North Carolina, Session 1866-7 (Raleigh: William E. Pell, 1867), doc. no. 1, p. 10. James L. Orr, Governor's Message, November 27, 1866, Journal of the House of Representatives of the State of South Carolina (Columbia: F.G. DeFontaine, 1866), 32-35.

73. Acts of the General Assembly of the State of Virginia passed at the Session of 1869-'70 (Richmond: James E. Goode, 1870), 413.

   Journal of the Constitutional Convention of the State of North Carolina (Raleigh Joseph W. Holden, 1868), 343.

   Journal of the House of Representatives of the General Assembly of the State of North Carolina at its Session of 1872-'73 (Raleigh: Stone and Uzzell, 1873), 260.298.

74. Infra, V, 184.

75. Proceedings of the Constitutional Convention of South Carolina (Charleston: Denny and Perry, 1868), 889-894, 899-902. Frederick A. Sawyer, Alonzo J. Ransier, Richard A. Cain, and Robert B. Elliott, who were members of Congress during debate on Sumner's civil rights bill, were members of this convention. Elliott and Cain defended Sumner's bill with reference to the Fourteenth Amendment (Supra, III, 95, 100).

76. Journal of the Proceedings of the Constitutional Convention of the People of Georgia (Augusta: E.H. Pughe, 1868), 151, 477-450, 482.

77. Charles J. Jenkins, Governor's Message, November 1, 1866, Journal of the House of Representatives of the State of Georgia (Milledgeville: J.W. Burke and Co., 1866), 7-11. Ibid, 61-68 (committee report). The Southern Recorder, November 6, 1866, 1.

78. Rufus B. Bullock, Governor's Message, July 24, 1868, Journal of the House of Representatives of the State of Georgia (Macon: J.W Burke and Co., 1666),'75-76.

79. The Southern Recorder, May 29, 1866, 2.

80. David S. Walker, Governor's Message, November 14, 1866, Journal of the Proceedings of the House of Representatives of the General Assembly of the State of Florida, at the 2D Session of the 14th General Assembly (Tallahassee: Dyke and Sarhawk, 1866), 11-17.

Benjamin G. Humphreys, Governor's Message, October 16, 1866, Journal of the Senate of the State of Mississippi (Jackson: J.J. Shannon and Co., 1866), 8. Ibid., 77-87 (Committee Report).

James W. Throckmorton, Governor's Message, August 18, 1866, Journal of the House of Representatives. Eleventh Legislature, State of Texas (Austin: The office of the State Gazette, 1866), 92-93. Ibid., 417-423.

81. Journal of the Senate of the State of Louisiana (Jackson: Kimball, Raymond and Co., 1870), 569. General Laws of the State of Texas (Austin: John Cardwell, 1873) 90.

82. Documents of the First Session of the Second Legislature of the State of Louisiana (New Orleans: J.O. Nixon, 1866), doc, no. 15, p. 2. This report referred to a house joint resolution, part of which concerned the condition of the freedmen. The resolution, however, is not recorded. The report said 'the action would be unnecessary in view of the humane provision of the law of Louisiana' (regarding the condition of the freedmen), but it did not define "the action."

83. The Daily Picayune, October 2, 1866, 3.

84. New Orleans Tribune, September 5, 1866, 1; October 14, 16, 1866 (Sumner's address in Boston October 4, 1866. Supra, III,80); October 25 1866, 1 (a report of the resolutions adopted by a Negro convention at Galesburg, Illinois-- that the Illinois legislature grant Negro suffrage and. that Negroes never cease to strive to acquire property and to get their children admitted to the public schools); November 6, 1866, 3 (comment that suffrage brings the desire for education).

85. Ibid., April 26, 1667 1. This idea was also expressed in the April 14, 1867 issue of the Tribune (p. 1). On three other occasions the paper defended integrated schools, but without reference to either the Civil Rights Act or the Fourteenth Amendment (April 21, 1867 1; May 9, 1867, 1; July 9, 1867, 1).

86. "Message of Governor H.C. Warmouth, Vetoing the Civil Rights Bill," <u>Louisiana Documents, 1867-1868</u> (New Orleans: A.L. Lee, 1868), 5-6.

87. <u>The Louisianian</u>, December 22, 1870, 1.

CHAPTER 6

STATE DEPARTMENTS OF EDUCATION AND THE FOURTEENTH AMENDMENT

Perhaps the most significant discussion on segregation during this reconstruction period came from those most responsible for the administration of state and county school systems. Less concerned with political struggles for the control of legislative bodies, they could express more freely than members of Congress and state legislatures their attitudes about the Fourteenth Amendment and Negro education. These attitudes, while not strictly related to the question of the intent of those responsible for the passage and ratification of the Amendment, do suggest the degree to which there was an association in contemporary thought between section one of the Amendment, on the one hand, and Negro education, on the other.

Various geographic sections of the country again reflect differing opinions, and as was evident in Chapter IV, concern about Negro education naturally varies in relation to the proportionate number of Negroes living in any given area. Thus in those states situated just north and west of the Border states there is more discussion and division of opinion regarding Negro education than there is in either of the extremes, the far Northern states and the

Southern and Border states, where a sparse and dense Negro population respectively, produced a relative degree of uniformity in thought regarding Negro education.

While there were differing opinions and practices in New England and the far Northern states, there was a predominate pattern of school integration.

The annual report on education in Massachusetts for the year 1865 expressed a sentiment that had characterized the administration of the state's schools for ten years: School law "requires the Public Schools of every grade to be entirely and absolutely, and as a matter of right, free to all the children on its soil, without distinction of sect, rank, color or race."[1] A reply to an inquiry sent in 1868 by the superintendent of education for Indiana[2] restated this policy: '...in Massachusetts there is <u>no distinction</u> between <u>white</u> and <u>colored citizens</u> in respect to any <u>right</u> or <u>privilege</u> conferred by law. They are literally and truly equal before the law, <u>in all respects</u>--Suffrage, Education, <u>etc., etc</u>. The only distinction is in social treatment.[3]

In reply to the same inquiry from Indiana the superintendent of education for Vermont simply stated that "neither constitution nor statute recognizes any distinctions based upon race or color."[4]

In Connecticut and Rhode Island at this time there was some concern about Negro education. This resulted in the Connecticut law of August, 1868, that incorporated school integration into state law, which had said nothing of Negro education prior to this time.[5] School integration was postponed in Rhode Island, however. In considering the "vexed question" of segregation the school board of Providence County expressed feelings torn between the "progressive spirit of the age" and what was thought "expedient in the present state of public opinion." Particularly during the past year (1869), said the report, had the board considered abolishing the separate Negro schools that had been established for over three decades. In the "best interest of the colored children," however, it was decided to keep the schools separate. Prejudice must soon yield to the rapidly changing sentiments of the people," concluded the report, and "then our public schools will be thrown open to all children and youth...without any distinction whatever of nationality or complexion."[6]

In New York, the establishment of schools for Negroes had been recognized by law since 1847.[7] By 1866 schools were either segregated or integrated, depending upon whether the local board felt there were enough Negroes in the area to warrant the construction of a separate school. Negroes were entitled by law to attend white schools, except where separate schools were established, said state superintendent Abram B. Weaver in 1868 in answer to the Indiana inquiry,[8] and this policy remained unchanged throughout the Reconstruction period.[9]

There was little reference to the Negro in the reports on education for Michigan, Wisconsin, and Minnesota. Undoubtedly the Negroes, who were included within the scope of public school law, were educated with the white children.[10] The response to the Indiana inquiry by Mark H. Dunnell of Minnesota said that Negro children in his state had "all the rights, privileges and immunities of white children. They are excluded from no educational rights. They are just as the white children in their opportunities?"[11]

In contrast to the more "liberal" policies existing in these Northern states was the segregation established in Nevada and California. Nevada law required Negroes to be educated in separate schools, but school boards were not required to organize them. By this provision Negroes were virtually deprived of an education, even though they were subject to taxation for the support of the public schools. In 1870 the state superintendent of education called attention to this "injustice"; his remarks, however, referred only to the immediate situation and did not suggest a belief that there had been a violation of the equality guaranteed by the Fourteenth Amendment.[12]

In California, until 1873, both segregation and integration were recognized, by law. Legislation in 1864 and 1866 excluded Negroes, Orientals, and Indians from the public schools unless the parents or guardians of ten or more such children applied for their admission. In this case separate schools were to be established. The law of 1866 went further than that of 1864, however, by allowing children of these minority groups to be educated with whites when there were not enough to make the organization of a separate school practical and when a majority of the parents of the children in the school involved gave their consent to integration. Then by the school, law of 1873 it was provided that the education of Negroes and Indians "must be provided for in separate schools," and again only upon application for such.[13] The only comment upon any of this legislation was in 1865 by state superintendent John Swett, who believed that provision for the separate education of Negroes, Indians, and Orientals was required by the dictates of justice and common humanity.

"If all classes pay taxes on their property for the support of schools," he said, "there is no reason why the children of all classes, whether white, black, tawny, or copper-colored, should not be educated."[14]

Only in these most Northern states of the Union was the predominate state policy one of integration, and while there was no direct reference to the Fourteenth Amendment there were statements similar to the expression of equality found in section one of the Amendment. The replies to the Indiana inquiry from Massachusetts and. Minnesota spoke of equality before the law and of the rights, privileges, and immunities of Negroes when speaking of school systems that educated Negro and white together. Further, as noted in Chapter IV, the integration of the schools in Connecticut seems particularly to be the result of the Amendment's demand for equality. Much less definite was the reference in Rhode Island to "the progressive spirit of the age" when considering integration of the schools. In its context, however, it suggests a belief that segregation was less than the equality demanded by that spirit. In Nevada and California, on the other hand, where segregation was required, two respective superintendents of education expressed the opinion that Negroes were entitled to an education simply because they paid school taxes.

There was a considerable degree of discussion about Negro education in the states from New Jersey to Kansas, between the more Northern states and the Border states. When there was a defense of either Negro education per se or integration there were also some expressions of concern for equality in language similar to that in section one of the Fourteenth Amendment. There were, further, two direct references to the Fourteenth Amendment.

New Jersey school law said nothing of race or color in 1865, and this was thought by the department of education to mean that Negroes were to receive an education.[15] Separate schools were established for them, and there was no opinion expressed that they should be integrated. In 1868 the report from Camden County noted that it was difficult to educate the Negroes because school funds could not support separate schools; consequently, Negro schools were open for only a few months in the year.[16]

In Pennsylvania, Negroes were educated in separate schools when there were at least twenty pupils living close to one another; otherwise, they were admitted into white schools. Negroes were not allowed to enter white schools where separate ones existed, however, wrote state superintendent C.R. Coburn in answer to the Indiana inquiry of 1868.[17] No one within the state department of education questioned this practice, and in 1870 the annual school report stated: "...the aim of our common school system is not exclusive; it knows no distinction of class or condition."[18]

There was some doubt cast upon existing policy in Ohio, however. Even though the school law of 1864 said that Negroes were to be educated in separate schools, it was the practice in many

areas to allow Negroes into white schools.[19] This was due to financial problems involved in maintaining separate schools. In 1871
state superintendent Thomas W. Harvey noted that "in its practical operations the school law of 1864 deprived many Negroes of
an education." The funds set aside for separate schools often were
not adequate to maintain them, he said, and the schools therefore
had to close early in the term. Also, in some areas all the school
funds were spent on white schools, thus keeping the Negro from
any public school education. The Superintendent then pleaded for
a change in the law: "No inequality in civil and political rights is
now recognized as existing between the different races and na-
tionalities of which the population of our State is composed.... If
education is of worth, and intelligence and morality the surest safe-
guards in a republic, equal and adequate means for culture should
be provided for all.... It is therefore respectfully recommended
that the statute requiring the establishment of separate schools
for colored youth, be so amended as to secure to them educational
advantages equal to those enjoyed by other youth."[20]

It was in this same year that the Ohio supreme court, upon
examination of the Fourteenth Amendment, declared, the constitutionality of separate Negro schools. "Substantially equal school
advantages" must be secured, however, said Judge Luther Day in
writing the unanimous decision.

The only subsequent change in school law came in 1873, when
it was provided that Negroes could attend white schools if the local
board approved this action.[21]

Negroes were not included in Indiana school law until 1869,
when provision was made for the establishment of separate
schools. Both the superintendents of education for 1866 and
1868 criticized the failure to provide for Negro education. In his
school report for 1866 George W. Hose spoke of the Negro as a
"new force" in society and then stated; "any force generated in, or
injected into, the social or political organism at once suggests the

necessity of guidance or control. Uncontrolled, evil if not ruin will ensue. But in a popular government like ours, human force in the aspect now under consideration, is more easily controlled for the good of society and the State, when the party possessing and exerting such force, is educated." The Superintendent than argued that existing state school law included the Negro because of its recognition that education was "essential to the preservation of a free government." He also suggested that legislation be passed requiring the organization of separate schools for Negroes when at least fifteen pupils resided "within attending distance" and requiring the school board to educate Negroes "in such manner" as they might provide when there were less than fifteen pupils "in any neighborbood."[22]

In 1868 superintendent Barnabas C. Hobbs was equally concerned about the neglect of Negro education and wrote other state superintendents in order to ascertain what "rights and privileges" were extended Negroes in their respective states. "Whatever distinction may have been made in the rights and privileges by our laws," said Hobbs, "have been set aside by the emendations of our National Constitution and. the 'Civil Rights Bill.' All citizens are now equal before the law."

The Superintendent then noted that while Negroes were taxed for the support of the public school system, they were denied its benefits and had to tax themselves additionally in order to raise money for school purposes. Said Hobbs: "The historian will find this a dark chapter in our history."[23]

In 1872 superintendent Milton C. Hopkins commented upon the success of the law of 1869 that provided for Negro education. Separate schools were established wherever Negroes were "congregated in sufficient numbers,' and the school terms were 'equal in duration to those of the other schools." In some cases, "by common consent," Negroes were admitted to white schools when they were few in number, said Hopkins, and when they were refused admittance the school board spent their proportion of the school revenue "to the best advantage" for their education.[24]

Illinois was also a state in which some doubt existed as to the statue of the Negro in relation to state school law. Until 1870 the Negro was not allowed by law to receive a public school education, although in some districts, when no objection was made, Negroes were admitted to the schools.[25]

Between 1870 and 1874 legislation said nothing of the Negro, but in practice school boards gradually accepted the responsibility of educating him. This was undoubtedly due in part to the efforts of state superintendent Newton Bateman, who strongly believed the Negro was included in Illinois school law. He also felt the segregation issue was one of "secondary importance" that should be settled by each school district as it thought best.

In his biennial report for 1867-1868 Bateman criticized existing law that excluded Negroes from the benefit of the public school system: "Let us expunge this last remaining remnant of the unchristian 'black laws' of Illinois, and proclaim in the name of God, and the Declaration of Independence, that all the school-going children of the State, without distinction, shall be equally entitled to share in the rich provisions of the free school system." The segregation question, he continued, was "entirely separate and distinct" from the one at hand and could safely be left to be determined by the respective districts and communities.... Only drive the spirit of caste from its entrenchments in the statute, giving all equal educational rights under the law, and the consequences will take care of themselves."[26]

It was Bateman's opinion in 1870 that Negroes were included within the scope of the article on education in the revised Illinois constitution of 1870. The article said: "The general assembly shall provide a thorough and efficient system of free schools, whereby all children of this state may receive a good common school education." Bateman commented: "There is no white, no black, no exception, distinction or discrimination in this language. Its scope is coextensive with the territorial limits of the state, and the boon which it provides is for every child in the state.' The Superintendent then restated his earlier views on the question of segregation. The issue was of "secondary importance and, he noted, had not been considered of enough consequence to be mentioned in the constitution. It was better, he believed, for legislation to say nothing on the subject. "It is one of those matters which involve no principle worth striving about, and which are best left to regulate themselves." He felt the school boards possessed the right to determine the way in which Negroes were to be educated, and if there were objection about either practice then the matter could be settled in court. He further believed that if the question did go to the court the decision would say that Negroes had the right to "demand the education," but not the right to "dictate as to the particular schools which they shall attend.[27]

In his report for 1871-1872 Bateman again wrote in defense of Negro education. He noted that some Negroes were deprived of an education by not being allowed to enter white schools in areas where there were no separate schools established. In other instances Negroes deprived, themselves of an education by refusing to attend the poor substitutes provided for them. The Superintendent felt the legislature should concern itself with this discrimination. "Is the right to vote so much more sacred than the right to be educated?" he asked.[28]

In 1874 Bateman quoted at length from his report for 1869-1870 and added that the segregation issue had been taken to court and decided as he had thought it would be. Be then referred to the Ohio supreme court case of Garnes v. McCann.[29] "What the [fourteenth] amendment plainly guarantees," concluded Bateman, "is that the two races shall be provided with equal public school advantages. This, it seems to me, is the only essential point--the only thing worth contending for. The schools provided for colored children must not be in any respect inferior to those provided for others...." If no separate schools existed in an area because of a sparse Negro population, he continued, then Negroes must be admitted to white schools, as had been decided in the Illinois case of Chase v. Stephenson (71 <u>Illinois Reports</u>, 383), when the state supreme court held that the construction of a separate school for two Negroes on the same lot with a white school was a "squandering of the public funds."[30]

To settle Bateman' a main contention throughout this period--that Negroes should be included within the state public school system--the legislature passed a bill in March, 18$, designed Ito protect colored children in their rights to attend public schools,"[3]

School law in Iowa in 1866 said there was to be no distinction made because of color in the public school system, but it took a state supreme court decision in April, 1868, to interpret this to mean integration. That same year state superintendent D. Franklin Wells answered the Indiana inquiry by stating that a man's rights and privileges were no longer determined "by the color of his skin" in the state of Iowa. Along with the Negro right to vote, to hold office, to possess property, and to be a part of the militia was the right to receive an education 'on the same footing with white citizens. Wells referred only to the Iowa constitution as the basin upon which this equality rested.[32]

In Nebraska, until 1873, there was little reference to the Negro in the annual reports on education. Evidently schools were either segregated or integrated depending upon the number of Negroes living in the area. In the city and. county reports for 1872 there was reference to a Negro school in Nebraska City, and in the same reports for 1874 one Negro pupil was reported in. Beatrice county and one in Bellevue county.[33]

School segregation became an issue in Kansas and was discussed at some length in the annual reports on education. By the school law of 1863 each school district was to settle the question for itself: "...to make such order as they may deem proper for the education of white and colored children, separately or otherwise, securing to them equal educational advantages."[34] In Kansas, then, three years before the consideration of the Fourteenth Amendment in Congress there was an expression of equality in the school law. Until 1867 the few comments about Negro education were generally related only to the fact that for the first time Negroes were receiving an education. That there was some difficulty in this movement is noted by a comment from the report on schools in Doniphan county for 1866: "A great embarrassment in our schools is the colored element. How shall the colored people be secured in their rights to the common schools of the State as prescribed by law? I think the law defective in not providing penalties for its infraction."[35]

For the years 1867-1869 the state superintendent of education, Peter McVicar, endeavored to secure the fulfillment of law regarding Negro education. He favored integration, but recognized separate schools if they did in fact provide "equal educational advantages," as the law stated. It will not do," he said, "to establish a graded school for white children and keep the colored children always in a primary department. It will not do to build fine edifices for the one class and crowd the other into poorly lighted and ill-ventilated, rooms." And in small school districts, said the Superintendent, there was no sense in even trying to support separate schools. Such a course was impractical and led only to "injury to all classes." "Why not permit all the children of the community, without distinction of condition or color, to enter our public schools together. It must come to this." McVicar also noted that some people were even advocating a policy whereby Negroes would be given only the amount collected from them in school taxes plus whatever amount might be collected from a tax on Negro property. Such a plan, said McVicar, would only deprive Negroes of an education because of their poor financial condition. "If colored children are human," he concluded, "give them the rights of humanity. If they are low, elevate them. If they have suffered privations, grant them now the equal advantages which the law provides."[36]

In his reports for 1868 and 1869 McVicar repeated his plea for equal school advantages for Negroes, and in his report for 1869 he also eliminated, the classification, of pupils by color, stating it was better for statistics to drop the discrimination respecting the color of persons of school ages."[37]

County school reports for the years under McVicar's administration reflect the trouble attending his attempt to secure equal school privileges for Negroes. In 1867 Doniphan and Morris counties reported strong public prejudice against integration, and in 1868 Ellsworth and Leavenworth counties reported that many Negroes were receiving no education because of pressure to keep them out of the white schools.[38] Attitudes of local school authorities also hindered McVicar's work. Said the report from Morris county in 1867: "...one ill-disposed negro, aided by vicious white persons, may destroy half a dozen schools in a county during a year." And in 1869 the report from Jefferson county similarly noted that "'negro on the brain'" had been the cause of the closing of three schools.[39]

Succeeding school reports recorded the existence of both integrated and segregated schools. There were also a few references to continued difficulties involved in educating the Negro.[40] Little comment upon the subject, however, indicates that state superintendents succeeding McVicar either felt the terms of law fulfilled or were not so concerned about Negro education as McVicar had been.

In 1874 the Kansas legislature passed a civil rights bill that forbade discrimination because of color in the public school system. A lack of either praise or protest of this bill within the annual reports on education suggests that it was not felt to contravene existing practice. Certainly there would have been comment if it had been thought to require integration, for the segregation issue was by no means settled by a universal backing of integration.

There was more concern for Negro education expressed in these states extending from Kansas to New Jersey than in any other area of the country. There was expression of the concept of equal school privileges for Negro and white in the reports on education for Ohio, Indiana, Illinois, and. Kansas. Also, it was said by a superintendent of schools for Pennsylvania that there was no distinction made in the Pennsylvania public schools because of color, and in Illinois and Iowa state superintendents Bateman and Wells referred to education as a right. In Indiana and Illinois Negroes were formally included in state school law for the first time during Reconstruction--1869 in Indiana and 1874 in Illinois. Other states in this area had made provision for Negro education prior to 1866.

In these statements of Negro equality there was one reference to the Civil Rights Act and the Fourteenth Amendment and one comment upon the Fourteenth Amendment. The former was by superintendent Hobbs of Indiana when noting the changes in national law regarding the guarantee of equal rights, and the latter was by Bateman of Illinois when discussing the Ohio case, Garnes V. McCann. Except for Iowa, however, in no state was it felt that this concept of equal school privileges for Negroes required integration, and usually separate schools were organized. Superintendents Harvey of Ohio and McVicar of Kansas, however, felt it necessary to urge integration when inadequate funds made it impossible to support separate schools. This concern over lack of financial support for separate Negro schools was also expressed in New Jersey and. Indiana, and in the latter state, until 1869, Negroes were able to collect school funds derived only by a self-imposed tax on their property.

A similar method of financing Negro education was instituted in Maryland and Kentucky by law, and in all of the Border states, unlike any other area during Reconstruction, schools were required to be segregated.

In his annual report to the legislature in 1865 state superintendent L. Van Bokkelen of Maryland proposed that the state establish schools for Negroes whenever "as many as twenty-five... claim the privilege of public instruction." These schools, said the Superintendent, should "in all respects be equal to the schools designed for the education of other children, and be subject in every particular to the same rules and regulations as to teachers, textbooks, school libraries, etc."[41] In 1866 Van Bokkelen spoke of the need to educate the Negro in order to keep him from "ignorance and vice." The Superintendent also believed that Negro and white should be educated separately because Negroes "could not mingle with the white children."[42]

Provision for Negro education was made by the legislature in 1868. Separate schools were to be established and supported from taxes paid by Negroes for school purposes and from any donations that might be made.[43] It was noted in the school report for 1871, however, that his arrangement was "practically worthless." The president of the state board of school commissioners, M.A. Newell, argued that education for the Negro was necessary because of his new status in society. If he was not educated, he said, he would be led to pauperism and crime by his freedom and possession of "civil and political rights."[44] Subsequent school law did not change this method of financing Negro education.[45]

Separate Negro schools were required in West Virginia by the revised constitution of 1872. This requirement, however, was simply a constitutional recognition of school segregation already established within the state.

In Kentucky, by an act of March 9, 1867, Negroes and mulattoes were to be subject to a special tax that would be used to support both Negro and mulatto paupers and. schools. This act further stated that "the trustees of each common school district in the county <u>may</u> cause a school to be taught in the district for the education of negro and mulatto children in said district.[46] It was this feature of the law that enabled school officials to ignore Negro education, and the state superintendent of education criticized this defeat of law and evasion, of duty .[47]

In his report for 1868 state superintendent Z. F. Smith answered an objection raised concerning a proposed increase in the state school tax. The objection was that if either the Fifteenth Amendment[48] were adopted or Kentucky reconstructed then either the schools might be integrated or Negroes would receive a pro rata amount of the school fund. Smith first noted that whenever the defeat of a measure was sought in the state the opposition appealed to existing prejudice against the Negro in order to gain its object. 'It matters not what party needs him [the Negro]," said Smith, 'or what desperate cause must be saved, as a last resort, he always comes handy. Whether he is wanted to rattle his heels on a political platform, or to dangle as a scarecrow from the top end of a liberty-pole, he is sure to turn up in the nick of time." The Superintendent then argued that even if the Fifteenth Amendment were adopted the Democratic vote of the state could control the combined Negro and Radical vote. "'But Kentucky may be reconstructed,' say these alarmists and croakers, 'and under military rule, the negroes may be admitted to school privileged ' Yes, and the world <u>may</u> come to and end in twelve months; and, therefore, farmers should put in no crops this spring," Smith retorted. Such "absurd folly" should not lead the state to vote for "<u>popular ignorance</u>," said the Superintendent. As long as the state continued under Democratic guidance there need be no fear that state institutions be changed contrary "to the wishes of the people."[49]

The following year the law of 1867 was repealed, leaving the Negro outside any state law related to education. Smith felt this a regrettable step by the legislature, and his successor, N.A.I.

Henderson, also criticized, this action. The Negro needed an education, he said, because of his possession of the ballot. There need be no integrated schools, he said; a separate system supported by Negro taxes would be sufficient.[50]

In 1874 provision for Negro education was reinstated into Kentucky law separate schools were to be organized and supported by taxes on Negro property, on licenses or deeds issued Negroes, on dogs owned by Negroes, by fines levied on Negroes, by a Negro poll tax, and by any money that might come from Congress. Henderson felt Congress should give the states money to support the Negro since it was Congress that had invested him with the franchise of American citizenship."[51]

Negroes in Missouri found state law more "liberal" than in Kentucky. By an act of February 20, 1865, the word "white" was stricken from Missouri school law; a general provision was also made for the education of Negroes in separate schools, on March 20, 1866, it was specifically provided that a separate school be constructed when there were at least twenty Negroes in an area; when there were fewer than twenty the money due them was to be spent as the local school board thought proper. "...in all other respects the terms and advantages of said schools shall be equal to others of the same grade in their respective township, cities, and villages," the law concluded.[52]

Both state superintendent T.A. Parker and his successor, John Montieth, commented upon the problem of educating the Negroes that lived in areas not supporting a separate school, and both suggested that Negroes be allowed to enter white schools. The matter had to be decided, by local authorities, however, said Montieth, since the law spoke only of separate schools. Integration was a question that confronted "prejudice," said the Superintendent, and appealed to "benevolence more than to law."[53]

In his report for 1874 Montieth criticized the congressional civil rights bill, which threatened to integrate the schools, but he did not feel the state school system should be "overthrown by direct action," as some thought necessary if the bill were passed. "The best interests of the colored people" lay in separate schools, said Montieth. They could succeed, however, only upon the basis of equal advantages to both classes.[54]

In the three Border states of Maryland, Kentucky, and Missouri, then, there was reference to the separate but equal doctrine--Maryland in 1865, Kentucky in 1868, and Missouri in 1865 and 1874. Significantly, therefore, there was reference to this doctrine prior to the passage of the Fourteenth Amendment. Also significant is the comment by state superintendent of Kentucky schools for 1868, to the effect that the Fourteenth Amendment might require integrated schools, or at least the equal distribution of school funds for a segregated system.

Other opinions about Negro education in the Border states--apart from hostility--reflect a belief in its necessity because of a new freedom. The state superintendent of education for Maryland in 1866 felt education necessary to keep the Negro from vice; the superintendent for 1871 referred to the extended suffrage as a reason for Negro education. Also in Kentucky, in 1871, the superintendent expressed concern for Negro education because of the elective franchise.

In the South, the vast majority of schools were segregated, and there was little comment upon either the question of Negro education per as or the segregation issue. There were scattered references to the separate but equal doctrine, and integration was felt necessary in Louisiana if there was to be an equality before the law between Negro and white.

School segregation was established by law in Arkansas July 23, 1868, and this provision remained unchanged throughout Reconstruction. In the biennial school report for 1868-1870 there was brief comment upon Negro education. When Congress endowed Negroes with "the rights of citizenship," said the report, then there was a great increase in the number of persons having a right to participate in "civil affairs" who were unable to read or write. Education was therefore necessary.[56]

The school system in Tennessee was also organized upon a basis of segregation. This was secured by legislation passed March 5, 1867.[57] In his report for 1874 state superintendent John N. Fleming criticized, the congressional civil rights bill because of the integration it would require in the schools. "The school law is absolutely impartial in its provisions as affecting the races," said Fleming; "the only distinction" made was the organization of separate schools, and this was for "the good health of both races," just as one might provide for the segregation of the sexes.[58]

A public school system was not instituted in Virginia until 1870, and schools here were also required to be segregated.[59] Only a few comments about Negro education appeared in the school reports between 1870 and 1875. In his report for 1871 state superintendent William H. Ruffner stated that the Negro laborer would be of greater economic value to the state if he were educated. He also felt education necessary because of the suffrage.[60] In the county reports for 1874 there were strong expressions of disapproval of the congressional civil rights bill because of fear of integration.[61]

Opposition to the civil rights bill was also expressed in the annual report on education for North Carolina in 1871. Superintendent Alexander McIver commented upon a letter he had received from Senator Augustus S. Merrimon, who had inquired the opinion of the Superintendent regarding the civil rights bill. McIver stated that he had replied by noting the universal opposition to integration within the state. The Superintendent then concluded in his report: "Whatever abstract ideas they [the Northerners] may entertain in regard to the absolute and total disregard of social distrc1ons in the school house, yet they would not desire to see the General Government do violence to public sentiment, and interfere in matters which appear to be exclusively within the province of State legislation.[62] Public schools in North Carolina had been segregated by law since March 1, 1873, and had been segregated in practice since their organization under Radical government.[63]

In South Carolina, the Radical constitution of 1868 seemed to indicate that schools were to be integrated by stating that "all public schools shall be free and open to all the children and youths of the State, without regard to race or color." In the county reports on education for 1869 there were several comments upon a proposed school bill, which, like the constitution, did not contain an explicit requirement for either segregation or integration. The reports from Clarendon, Edgefield, Fairfield, Greenville, Kershaw, Marlboro, Pickens, and Spartenbury counties defended segregation, usually with the comment that Negroes preferred separate schools.[64] The report from Kershaw county said that Negroes desired only "a fair and equal share of the public school fund.[65] There was just one defense of integration. Said the report from Georgetown county: All citizens "should be as one harmonious and united whole."[66] The school bill in question passed the legislature February 16, 1870, and the schools continued to be organized upon a segregated basis.[67]

Public schools in Georgia and Florida evidently were also segregated[68] as were the schools in Alabama and Mississippi.[69] In Mississippi, and perhaps also in Alabama, Florida, and Georgia, however, this segregation was not required by law. Reports from Itawamba and. Jasper counties in Mississippi for 1871 indicate that integrated schools may have existed in some areas of the state. The report from Itawamba county stated that a sparse Negro population made it difficult to establish a separate school and that the board had tried to get Negroes to attend school even if a separate school was established. The report from Jasper county stated that no integrated schools existed within the county and that residents there did not desire them.[70] Also, in Congress, May 22, 1874, in defense of Sumner's civil rights bill, Senator Henry R. Pease stated that Negroes could legally enter white schools in Mississippi.[71]

A few other comments from Mississippi county school reports for 1871 and 1872 are of interest. In defense of Negro education John Williams of Madison county said it was better to leave the Negro in slavery than to make him a citizen and then leave him in ignorance. Similarly, William B. Redmond of Amite county noted that the education of Negroes was necessary because of the "responsibility imposed by their new condition."[72] E. H. Osgood of Wilkerson county felt Negroes were "rightfully entitled to the same free public school advantages" belonging to white children, and Walter Gould. of Montgomery county said that "equal facilities to both races" must be secured and that there must be "no distinction made in salaries of teachers of either race of equal grade."[73]

The separate but equal doctrine also characterized the organization of schools in Texas. When Radical government was instituted in Texas, state school law was partial to the white population. Negro education could be supported only by a special tax levied upon them by the legislature. Radical school law eliminated, this distinction by simply providing for the education of all youth without stating any special provisions or conditions regarding Negro eduoation.[74] Negroes were educated in separate schools, however, and this practice became formalized in law May 23, 1873, when the legislature repassed a bill, requiring school segregation over the governor's veto[75] Both before and after 1873 it was stated that Negroes had a right to an equal share of the school funds.[76]

The separate but equal doctrine was not considered satisfactory by the Radical government in Louisiana, however. By the constitution of 1868 school integration was required.[77] In his school report for 1869 state superintendent Thomas W. Conway acknowledged the correctness of the state's required school integration: "A republican State can make no distinction between those who are equally citizens, nor can any humiliating condition be made in the bestowement of benefits to which all have an equal claim." "Reason and conscience" would ultimately prevail over prejudice, said Conway. In the meantime, however, prejudice was most real, and it was necessary to recognize its existence if the schools were not to collapse by forcing integration upon communities not desiring it. Education was the first aim, he noted, and the segregation issue was subordinate to it. "For the present," therefore, it was better to let the question be settled by the "unconstrained choice of those immediately interested." At the same time, however, he, as state superintendent, would continue to make clear to local authorities that the law demanded integration.[78]

In his report for 1871 Conway stated that "the principle of mixed schools" had been vindicated. "As a rule," said the Superintendent, "the children have chosen to attend schools made up principally of those of their own race," but in many schools both white and Negro were being educated together. A remaining difficulty, noted a report from a subordinate official, was the education of the "poor whites." The "planter aristocracy" took care of their own education, "intelligent white parents" sent their children to school with Negroes, but the "poor whites," through prejudice, refused to attend school with Negroes.[79]

In December, 1874, integration was challenged in New Orleans. Eleven Negro girls went to a white girls' high school to take entrance examinations for admission into the school, and, in protest, the white girls left the school. This episode was repeated at another white girls' high school when other Negro girls went there to take entrance examinations. Then boys from a white boys' high school went to the girls' schools to keep the Negro girls out by force, and eventually several groups of white boys went about to keep Negroes out of the grammar schools. This resulted in a fight and the death of a Negro man. No one was prosecuted, and the issue was left to be settled by the school authorities. While the Negro girls were given an opportunity to show their ability to pass the required examinations, they were not allowed to enter the white schools.[80]

In his report for 1875 state superintendent William G. Brown noted that the trouble in New Orleans had spread to other communities, and, he aptly summed up the state of affairs when he wrote, "The whole State of Louisiana sneezes when New Orleans takes snuff.[81] And a particularly strong dose brought about the collapse of integrated schools."

There was no reference to the Fourteenth Amendment in any of these school reports for Louisiana. The only comment upon the need for integration was the abatement by Conway in 1869--that "a republican State can make no distinction between those who are equally citizens." That he spoke of integration when stating this opinion, however, is of particular importance, since other Southern state departments of education believed that separate but equal schools fulfilled the newly established equality between Negro and white. The State superintendent of education for Tennessee had said in 1871 that no distinction existed between white and black except that they were educated separately, and in a county report from South Carolina for 1869 there was an expression of the opinion that Negroes deserved an equal share of the school fund. Similar statements were recorded in county reports from Mississippi for 1871 and 1872, and. in Texas the superintendents of education for 1871 and 187 spoke of Negro "educational rights," but within the framework of segregation. In none of these statements was there reference to the Fourteenth Amendment.

The only other comments in the South upon the desirability of integration were in South Carolina and Mississippi, and these also contained, no reference to the Amendment. In the former state a county report said that integration was necessary in order to enable white and black to live together harmoniously, and in Mississippi the officials of one county spoke of the difficulties involved in segregation because of the few Negro pupils in the area.

While integration was required in Louisiana during the recon-struction period, segregation was required in Tennessee (1867), Arkansas (1868), and Virginia (1870) and became formalized in law in North Carolina (1873) and Texas (1873) toward the end of Reconstruction.

Statements in the South concerning a rationale for Negro ed-ucation *per se* referred to the need for education because of the Negro's new status within society. A school report for Virginia in 1870 spoke particularly of the suffrage, while reports from Arkansas and Mississippi between 1870 and 1872 referred general-ly to the new freedom of the Negro. In no Southern state was there either reference to the Fourteenth Amendment when speaking of Negro education *per se* or statement of the idea that provision for Negro education followed because of a demand for civil equality.

To review, then, the relation between the concept of equality before the law and the ideas about Negro education during recon-struction, it is to be noted that there was an endorsement of equal Negro rights in the schools in Massachusetts, Iowa, Kansas, and Maryland prior to 1866. Similar expressions of equality in edu-cational advantage were expressed in or after 1866, but without specific reference to the Fourteenth Amendment, in the follow-ing states: Connecticut, Rhode Island, Minnesota, Pennsylvania, Ohio, Missouri, Tennessee, South Carolina, Mississippi, Texas, and. Louisiana. In two instances, in Indiana and Illinois, there was a consideration of both the Civil Rights Act and the Fourteenth Amendment in this question of the guarantee of equal school rights, and in one state, Kentucky, it was thought the Fourteenth Amendment might require either integration or equality in segregation.

These various expressions of equality occurred both in states where schools were integrated and in states where they were separate. They were integrated in Massachusetts, Connecticut, Minnesota, Iowa, and Louisiana. They were encouraged to be integrated in Ohio and Kansas when separate schools could not be maintained, and the separate schools in Rhode Island were thought to be less than the equality required by the spirit of the times. The thought that schools be equal while separate, on the other hand, was expressed in Pennsylvania, Ohio, Illinois, Indiana, Kansas, Maryland, Missouri, Tennessee, South Carolina, Mississippi, and Texas.

What can be concluded is the obvious. All these expressions of civil equality were either similar or identical to the statement of that guarantee within the first section 19 of the Fourteenth Amendment. Negro education was thought by many superintendents of education to be included within the concept of equality before the law. There was a distinct division of thought, however, regarding the definition of that equality. Some supported integration, others segregation.

FOOTNOTES: CHAPTER VI

State Departments of Education and the Fourteenth Amendment

1. "Twenty-Ninth Annual Report of the Board of Education," Public Documents of Massachusetts: Being the Annual Reports of Various Public Officers and Institutions for the Year 1865 (Boston: Wright and Potter, 1866), I, doc, no. 2, p. 70.

2. The superintendent of education for Indiana was concerned about the lack of provision for Negro education in Indiana law. In order to determine a policy for his own state he wrote to inquire of existing practices in other Northern states. There were no replies from Maine, New Hampshire, Connecticut, and Wisconsin.

3. Sixteenth Report of the Superintendent of Public Instruction for the State of Indiana (Indianapolis: Alexander H. Conner, 1869), 24.

4. Loc. cit.

5. "Annual Report of the Superintendent of Common Schools to the General Assembly," Public Documents of the Legislature of Connecticut at the May Session, 1869 (New Haven: Tuttle, Morehouse and Taylor, 1869) 218.

6. Third Annual Report on Public Schools in Rhode Island Made to the General Assembly at the January Session A.D. 1870 (Providence: Providence Press Company, 1870), 36.

7. Samuel S. Randall, The Common School System of the State of New York (Troy: Johnson and Davis, 1851), 230.

8. "Twelfth Annual Report of the Superintendent of Public Instruction of the State of New York," Documents of the Assembly of the State of New York (Albany: C. Wendell, 1866), V, doc. no. 90, pp. 76, 120, 322.

   Sixteenth Report of the Superintendent of Public Instruction for the State of Indiana (Indianapolis: Alexander H. Conner, 1869), 25.

9. "Fifteenth Annual Report of the Superintendent of Public Instruction of the State of New York," <u>Documents of the Assembly of the State of New York</u> (Albany: The Argus Company, 1869), VI, doc, no. 92, pp. 76, 197

'Twentieth Annual Report of the Superintendent of Public Instruction of the State of New York," <u>Documents of the Assembly of the State of New York</u> (Albany: The Argus Company, 1874), V, doc. no. 66, p. 80.

10. 'Twenty-Ninth Annual Report of the Superintendent of Public Instruction of the State of Michigan, with Accompanying Documents, for the Year 1865," <u>Joint Documents of the State of Michigan for the Year 1865</u> (Lansing: John A. Kerr and Co., 1865), 39-40.

"Annual Report of the Superintendent of Public Instruction of the State of Wisconsin for the Year Ending August 31st, 1867," <u>Wisconsin Documents</u>, 1867 (Madison: Atwood and Rublee, 1867), 786.

<u>Sixteenth Report of the Superintendent of Public Instruction for the State of Indiana....</u>, 26, 27.

11. <u>Ibid</u>., 27.

12. A. N. Fisher,"First Biennial Report of the Superintendent of Public Instruction for the School Years 1869 and 1870, <u>The Journal of the Senate During the Fifth Session of the Legislature of the State of Nevada, 1871</u> (Carson City: Charles L. Perkins, 1861), 14.

13. <u>School Law</u> (Sacramento: O.M. Clayes, 1864) 22. <u>Revised School Law</u> (Sacramento: O.M. Clayes, 1866), 18.

<u>Provisions of the Political Code Relative to Public Schools</u> (Sacramento: T.A. Springer, 1873), 21.

14. John Swett, "First Biennial Report of the Superintendent of Public Instruction of the State of California, for the School Year 1864 and 1865," <u>Appendix to Journals of Senate and Assembly of the Sixteenth Session of the Legislature of the</u>

State of California (Sacramento: O.M. Clayes, 1866), II, doc, no. 1, p. 57.

15. "Annual Report of the Superintendent of Public Schools of the State of New Jersey for the Year 1865," Documents of the Ninetieth Legislature of the State of New Jersey (New Brunswick: J.F. Babcock, 1866), 392.

16. "Annual Report of the State Board of Education," Documents of the Ninety-Third Legislature of the State of New Jersey, (Hudson City; William D. McGregor, 1869), 657.

17. Sixteenth Report of the Superintendent of Public Instruction for the State of Indiana (Indianapolis: Alexander T. Conner, 1869), 25.

18. "'Report of the Superintendent of Common Schools of the Commonwealth of Pennsylvania for the School Year Ending June 6, 1870," Reports of the Heads of Departments Transmitted to the Governor of Pennsylvania (Harrisburg: B. Singerly, 1871), xxiv.

19. "Seventeenth Annual Report of the State Commissioner of Common Schools to the General Assembly of the State of Ohio for the School Year Ending August 31, 1870," Message and Annual Reports for 1870 Made to the Fifty-Ninth General Assembly of the State of Ohio (Columbus: Nevins and Myers, 1871), II, 694.

20. Thomas W. Harvey, "Eighteenth Annual Report of the State Commissioner of Common Schools to the General Assembly of the State of Ohio for the School Year Ending August 31, 1871," Message and Annual Reports for 1871 Made to the Sixtieth General Assembly of the State of Ohio (Columbus: Nevins and Myers, 1872), II, 664.

21. "Twenty-Second Annual Report of the State Commissioner of Common Schools to the General Assembly of the State of Ohio for the School Year Ending August 31, 1875," Annual Reports for 1875Made to the Sixty-Second General Assembly of the State of Ohio (Columbus: Nevins and. Myers, 1876), II, 1060.

22. George W. Hoss, <u>Fourteenth Report of the Superintendent of Public Instruction for the State of Indiana</u> (Indianapolis: Samuel 14. Douglas, 1866), 49-51.

23. Barnabas C. Hobbs, <u>Sixteenth Report of the Superintendent of Public Instruction for the State of Indiana</u> (Indianapolis: Alexander H. Conner,1869), 23.

24. Milton B. Hopkins, <u>Twentieth Report of the Superintendent of Public Instruction for the State of Indiana</u> (Indianapolis R.J. Bright, 1872), 119.

25. <u>Sixteenth Report of the Superintendent of Public Instruction for the State of Indiana</u> (Indianapolis: Alexander H. Conner, 1869), 26.. In answer to the Indiana inquiry the superintendent of schools for Chicago reported that a separate Negro school had been opened in 1867, but had failed. Since 1865 Negroes had been allowed to enter the public schools "on an equality with other children." This arrangement proved to be more satisfactory than the "separate system," said the superintendent (<u>Loc. cit</u>.).

26. Newton Bateman, "Seventh Biennial Report of the Superintendent of Public Instruction 1867-1868," <u>Reports Made to the General Assembly of Illinois at its Twenty-Sixth Session</u> (Springfield: Illinois Journal Printing Office, 1869), II, 21.

27. Newton Bateman, "Eighth Biennial Report of the Superintendent of Public Instruction of the State of Illinois 1869-1870," <u>Report made to the General Assembly of Illinois at its Seventy-Seventh Session</u> (Springfield: Illinois Journal Printing Office, 1871), I, 355-356.

28. Newton Bateman, "Ninth Biennial Report of the Superintendent of Public Instruction 1871-1872," <u>Reports Made to the General Assembly of Illinois at its Twenty-Eighth Session</u> (Springfield: State Journal Steam Print, 1873), I, 118.

29. Bateman also referred to a New York case in 1873 that upheld separate Negro schools upon a study of the Fourteenth

Amendment. He gave no details of this case, however, and no reference to it has been found in other sources.

30. Newton Bateman, Tenth Biennial Report of the Superintendent of Public Instruction of the State of Illinois (Springfield: 1874), 43-48. Bateman concluded this report by summarizing the results of an inquiry sent by him to the local school boards. He asked them about their policies regarding Negro education and found a considerable degree of variety in practice—segregation, integration, and both segregation and integration. He felt this diversity strengthened his opinion that it was better to leave the issue with local authorities so long as educational advantages for white and black were always kept equal (Ibid., 49-50).

31. Journal of the Senate of the Senate of the Twenty-Eighth General Assembly of the State of Illinois (Springfield: State Journal Steam Print, 1874), 528.

32. Sixteenth Report of the Superintendent of Public Instruction for the State of Indiana (Indianapolis: Alexander H. Conner, 1869), 27-28.

33. Third Annual Report of the State Superintendent of Public Instruction to the Governor of Nebraska for the year December 31st, 1872 (Des Moines: Mills and Co., 1872), 124.

   Sixth Annual Report of the Superintendent of Public Instruction to the Governor of Nebraska for the Year Ending December 31st, 1874 (Lincoln: Journal Company, 1874), 206, 208.

34. Laws and Forms Relating to Common Schools in the State of Kansas (Leavenworth: Bulletin Book and Job Printing House, 1867), 42-43.

35. Sixth Annual Report of the Superintendent of Public Instruction of the State of Kansas (Leavenworth: Bulletin Book and Job Printing Office, 1567), 22.

36. Peter McVicar, Report of Superintendent of Public Instruction (Topeka, 1867), 49-51.

37. Peter McVicar, <u>Eighth Annual Report of the Superintendent of Public Instruction of the State of Kansas</u> (Topeka, 1868), 4.

    Peter McVicar, <u>Ninth Annual Report of the Superintendent of Public Instruction</u> (Topeka: S.S. Prouty, 1870), 3.

38. "Reports of County Superintendents," <u>Report of Superintendent of Public Instruction</u> (Topeka, 187), 81, 90.

    "Reports of County Superintendents," <u>Eighth Annual Report....</u>, 100, 105.

39. "Reports of County Superintendents," <u>Report of Superintendent of Public Instruction</u> (Topeka, 1867), 90.

    "Reports of County Superintendents," <u>Ninth Annual Report....</u>, 138.

40. <u>Eleventh Annual Report of the Department of Public Instruction of the State of Kansas</u> (Topeka: S.S. Prouty, 1871), 15).

    <u>Thirteenth Annual Report of the Department of Public Instruction of the State of Kansas</u> (Topeka: S.S. Prouty, 1873), 140.

    Fourteenth Annual Report of the Department of Public Instruction of the State of Kansas (Topeka: S.S. Prouty, 1974), 45.

41. L. Van Bokkelen, "Report of the State Superintendent of Public Instruction to the General Assembly of Maryland.," Journal of the Proceedings of the House of Delegates, January Session, 1865 (Annapolis: Richard P. Bayly, 1865), doc. "P," 66-67.

42. L. Van Bokkelen, "First Report of the State Superintendent of Public Instruction to the Governor of Maryland," <u>Journal of the Proceedings of the House of Delegates, Extra Session</u>, 1866 (Annapolis: Haverstick and Longneckers, 1866), doc. "E," 21, 22.

43. The Public Documents of the House of Delegates of Maryland January Session, 1868 (Annapolis: Wm Thompson of R., 1868), doc. "X," 37.

44. M. A. Newell, "Report of the Board of State School Commissioners," Journal of the Proceedings of the Senate of Maryland, January Session, 1872 (Annapolis: Wm. Thompson of R., 1872), doc. "V," 11-13.

45. Report of the State Board of Education Showing the Condition of the Public Schools of Maryland (Annapolis: L.F. Colton and Co., 1873), 9. It was noted in this report that there was difficulty in securing teachers for the Negro schools that were established. (Ibid., 18).

46. "Annual Report of the Superintendent of Public Instruction of Kentucky for the School Year Ending December 3, 1867," Kentucky Documents, 1867 (Frankfort, 1868), II, doc. no. 31, p. 276. Italics mine.

47. Z. F. Smith, Annual Report of the Superintendent of Public Instruction of Kentucky for the School Year Ending December 3, 1867 (Frankfort: Kentucky Yeoman Office, 1868), 42.

48. It was the Fifteenth Amendment to which the Superintendent referred, and not the Fourteenth. He undoubtedly meant the Fourteenth, however, since Congress did not consider and pass the Fifteenth Amendment until 1869.

49. Z. F. Smith, Annual Report of the Superintendent of Public Instruction of Kentucky for the School Year Ending December 31, 1868 (Frankfort: S.I.M. Major, 1869), 23-24.

50. Z. F. Smith, "Annual Report of the Superintendent of Public Instruction of Kentucky for the School Year Ending June 30, 1871, Kentucky Documents, 1871 (Frankfort, 1872), II, doc, no. 16, pp 99-100.

H.A.M. Henderson, "Annual Report of the Superintendent of Public Instruction of Kentucky for the School Year Ending

June 30, 1872," <u>Kentucky Documents, 1872</u> (Frankfort, 1872), I, doc. no. 2, p. 46.

51. "Annual Report of the Superintendent of Public Instruction of Kentucky for the School Year Ending June 30, 1874," <u>Kentucky Documents, 1874</u>. (Frankfort, 1875), I doc. no. 1, p. 29.

H.A.M. Henderson, "Annual Report of the Superintendent of Public Instruction of Kentucky for the School Year Ending June 30, 1875," <u>Kentucky Documents, 1875</u> (Frankfort, 1876), I, doc, no. 3, p. 106.

52. <u>Laws of the State of Missouri Passed at the Regular Session of the Twenty-Third General Assembly</u> (Jefferson City: W.A. Curry, 1865), 125-126.

<u>Laws of the State of Missouri Passed at the Adjourned Session of the Twenty-Third General Assembly</u> (Jefferson City: Emory S. Foster, 1866), 177.

53. T.A. Parker, <u>Fourth Report of the Superintendent of Public Schools of the State of Missouri</u> (Jefferson City: Horace Wilcox, 1870), 37.

John Montieth, <u>Seventh Report of the Superintendent of Public Schools of the State of Missouri</u> (Jefferson City: Regan and Carter, 1873), 45.

54. John Montieth, <u>Ninth Report of the Superintendent of Public Schools of the State of Missouri</u> (Jefferson City: Regan and Carter, 1875), 18.

55. <u>Journal of the Senate of Arkansas</u> (Little Rock: Price and Barton, 1869), 239.

<u>Journal of the Assembly of the State of Arkansas at Their Seventeenth Session</u> (Little Rock: John G. Price, 1868, 1870), I, 527.

56. Biennial Report of the Superintendent of Public Instruction (Little Rock, 1870), 5.

There was also reference to the fact that the state had taken over the schools operated by the Freedmen's Bureau (<u>Ibid.</u>, 9).

Almost all Freedmen's Bureau schools were established upon a segregated basis, and it was generally felt that this arrangement was no violation of equality before the law. A statement by Brevet Lt. Col. Edwin Beecher in 1869 regarding schools in Alabama was typical of the general sentiment: ...no distinction is made in the law between white and colored children, except that they are to be educated in separate schools, unless the full consent of the whites is obtained for a mixed school. The benefits of the law extend to one race as well as another." John W. Alvord, Eighth Semi-Annual Report on Schools For Freedmen, July 1, 1860 (Washington: Government Printing Office, 1869) one criticism of segregation in the semi-annual reports on the freedmen's schools. In 1870 John M. Langston of Kentucky wrote that the separate system 'must eventually fail,' since it was "abnormal" and "doubly expensive." Also, the system absolutely failed to educate Negro and white in such a way as to enable them to live together "harmoniously as fellow citizens and neighbors." John W. Alvord, Tenth Semi-Annual Report on Schools for Freedmen, July 1, 1870 (Washington: Government Printing Office, 1869), 39. There were only a few comments about why the Negro should be educated, and these were related to the extended suffrage, as, for example, a statement by Edwin Beecher in 1869: "...with universal suffrage conceded, surely the freedmen's vote should be intelligent." (John W. Alvord, Eighth Semi-Annual Report..., 3).

57. First Report of the Superintendent of Public Instruction of the State of Tennessee. (Nashville: Edgar Grisham, 1869), 5.

58. John M. Fleming, "Annual Report of John N. Fleming, State Superintendent of Public Instruction for Tennessee, for the Scholastic Year Ending August 31, 1874," Appendix to the Journal of the House of Representatives First Session, Thirty-Ninth General Assembly of the State of Tennessee (Nashville: Tavel, Eastman, and Howell, 1875), 26.

59. <u>Acts of the General Assembly of the State of Virginia Passed at the Session of 1869-'70</u> (Richmond: James E. Goode, 1870), 413.

60. William H. Ruffner, "First Annual Report of the Superintendent of Public Instruction for the Year Ending August 31, 1871," <u>Annual Reports of Officer's Boards and Institutions of the Commonwealth of Virginia for the Year Ending September 30, 1871</u> (Richmond: R.F. Walker, 1871), 106-108, 122.

61. "Fourth Annual Report of the Superintendent of Public Instruction for the Year Ending August 31, 1874," <u>Annual Reports of Officers Boards and Institutions of the Commonwealth of Virginia for the Year Ending September 30, 1874</u> (Richmond: R.F. Walker, 1874), 43, 44, 45, 46, 47, 48, 50, 51.

62. Alexander McIver, "Report of the Superintendent of Public Instruction," <u>Executive and Legislative Documents Laid before the General Assembly of North Carolina, Session 1874-'75</u> (Raleigh: Josiah Turner, 1875), doc. no. 5, p. 64.

63. Journal of the House of Representatives of the General Assembly of the State of North Carolina at its Session of 1872-'73 (Raleigh: Stone and Uzzel, 1873), 260, 298, 576.

"Report of Superintendent of Public Instruction," <u>Executive and Legislative Documents Laid Before the General Assembly of North Carolina, Session 1869-'70</u> (Raleigh: Jo. W. Holden, 1870), doc. no. 6, pp. 53-55.

64. "Report of the State Superintendent of Education," Reports and Resolutions of the General Assembly. South Carolina, 1869-1870 (Columbia, 1870), 466, 467-468, 469, 473, 576, 480, 481, 483.

65. Ibid., 476.

66. Ibid., 471.

67. "Third Annual Report of the State Superintendent of Education of the State of South Carolina," Reports and Resolutions of the General Assembly of the State of South Carolina at the Regular

Session, 1871-'72 (Columbia: Republican Printing Company, 1872). This and succeeding reports contained no reference to any integration. School statistics were categorized to indicate Negro children, white children, Negro teachers, and white teachers.

68. It is difficult to determine the state of Negro education for these states because so few records are available for examination. Documents studied refer only to separate Negro schools.

First Annual Report of the State School Commissioner of the State of Georgia (Atlanta, 1871), 12, 13.

The Georgia school report for 1883-1884 contains a chart listing the enrollment of students by color for the years 1871-1883. Report of the State School Commissioner of Georgia to the General Assembly (Atlanta: Jos. P. Harrison and Co., 1884), 3.

69. "Report of the Superintendent of Public Instruction of the State of Alabama," Alabama Documents, 1869-1870 (Montgomery, 1870), 7, 8, 9, 10.

"Report of Joseph Hodgson, Superintendent of Public Instruction," Alabama Documents, 1873. (Montgomery: W.W. Screws, 1871), 39-81.

Annual Report of the Superintendent [of] Public Education for the State of Mississippi for the Year Ending December 31, 1871 (Jackson: Kimball, Raymond and Co., 1872), 132.

Annual Report of the Superintendent [of] Public Education for the State of Mississippi for the Year Ending December 31, 1872 (Jackson: Kimball, Raymond and Co., 1873), 240.

70. Annual Report of the Superintendent [of] Public Education for the State of Mississippi for the Year Ending December 31, 1871 (Jackson: Kimball, Raymond and Co., 1872), 41, 44.

71. May 22, 1874, Congressional Record, 43 Cong., 1 sess., if, 4154. Pease had been the state superintendent of education in Mississippi prior to his term in Congress.

72. <u>Annual Report of the Superintendent [of] Public Education for the state of Mississippi for the Year Ending December 31, 1871….</u>, 68.

   <u>Annual Report of the Superintendent [of] Public Education for the State of Mississippi for the Year Ending December 31, 1872</u> (Jackson: Kimball, Raymond and Co., 1873), 118.

73. <u>Annual Report of the Superintendent [of] Public Education for the State of Mississippi for the Year Ending December 31, 1871…</u>, 114.

   <u>Annual Report of the Superintendent [of] Public Education for the State of Mississippi for the Year Ending December 31, 1872…</u>, 192.

74. <u>First Annual Report of the Superintendent of Public Instruction of the State of Texas, 1871</u> (Austin: J. G. Tracy, 1872), 30-34.

   <u>General Laws of the State of Texas</u> (Austin: Traoy, Siemering and Co., 1870), 114.

75. <u>First Annual Report…</u>, 50.

   <u>General Laws of the State of Texas</u> (Austin: John Cardwell, 1873), 90.

76. <u>First Annual Report…</u>, 52.

   Fourth Annual Report of the Superintendent of Public Instruction of the State of Texas for the Scholastic Year Ending August 31, 1874. (Houston: A.C. Gray, 1874), 12, 69.

77. In 1867 provision had been made for the establishment of separate Negro schools in New Orleans and Jefferson. "Report of the State Superintendent of Public Education for 1867 and 1868," <u>Louisiana Documents 1867-1868</u>, (New Orleans: A.L. Lee, 1869), 10-12.

78. Thomas W. Conway, "Annual Report of the State Superintendent of Public Instruction for 1869, to the General Assembly of Louisiana," <u>Louisiana Documents, 1869-1870</u> (New Orleans; A.L. Lee, 1870), 11-13.

79. Thomas W. Conway, Annual Report of the State Superintendent of Public Education, Thomas W. Conway, to the General Assembly of Louisiana for the Year 1871, Louisiana Documents 1871-1872 (New Orleans: The Republican Office, 1572), 47; 120.

80. William G. Brown, "Annual Report of the State Superintendent of Public Education, William G. Brown, to the General Assembly of Louisiana for the Year 1874," Documents of the First Session of the Fourth Legislature of the State of Louisiana (New Orleans: The Republican Office, 1875), 1-lxxvi. Brown's account of the affair was taken from reports of the episode appearing in The Daily Picayune, December 11-19, 1874. The paper simultaneously carried editorials condemning the Negro efforts.

William G. Brown, "Annual Report of the State Superintendent of Public Education, William G. Brown, to the General Assembly of Louisiana for the Year 1875," Louisiana Documents 1875-1876 (New Orleans: The Republican Office, 1876), 149.

81. William G. Brown, "Annual Report of the State Superintendent of Public Education, William G. Brown, to the General Assembly of Louisiana for the Year 1875," op. cit., 32.

CHAPTER 7

SUMMARY: THE STATES: 1866-1875

W hat, then, can be said of the States in considering the intent of the framers of the Fourteenth Amendment with regard to the question of separate Negro schools? In ratifying the Amendment most men in the state legislatures, like the majority in Congress in 1866, either did not feel Negro education included within the scope of section one or did not consider the possibility of their being related. That some thought the two related, however, is evident since there was expression of this idea at the state level during this time.

At the time the Amendment was being ratified and in the years just after its ratification several state legislatures included the Negro in state school law for the first time. This effort generally seems not to be related to the Amendment's demand for equality, however. The incorporation of the Fourteenth Amendment into law and the inclusion of the Negro in state school law appear to be two events produced by the same cause--the need to give the Negro more than just a raw freedom. In states that had provided for Negro education prior to 1866 there was generally no change in policy governing the education of Negroes, which included everything from required segregation to required integration. This again suggests either that the Fourteenth Amendment was not considered relevant to the segregation issue or that existing practice was felt compatible with the Amendment's requirement for equality before the law.

There are two notable exceptions to this conclusion, however. Connecticut school law was changed in August, 1868, to require integration, when previously it had said nothing of Negro education. This seems particularly to be the result of the requirement for equality as expressed in section one of the Fourteenth Amendment. Another specific correlation between the two seems evident in Louisiana, where, in contrast to all other Southern states, schools were required to be integrated. In neither of these cases, however, is it perfectly clear that the Fourteenth Amendment itself was the cause of the integration.

Three similar exceptions also appear within the reports from the state departments of education. An Indiana superintendent believed the Civil Rights Act and. the Fourteenth Amendment required the inclusion of the Negro within State school law. An Illinois superintendent referred to the consideration of the Fourteenth Amendment in the Ohio case of Garnes v. McCann when defending the separate but equal doctrine. And in Kentucky, the superintendent believed the Amendment might require either integrated schools or separate schools drawing equally from the school funds.

In other state departments of education there was also a concern that there be an equality before the law in the education of Negro and white, but there was no specific reference to the Fourteenth Amendment. That education was generally considered by many school officials to be within the concept of civil equality, however, is significant. The two subjects, then, cannot be considered so distinct and separate as other evidence indicates. Also, support given to the concept of equality before the law occurred both in states where schools were segregated and in those where they were integrate. It cannot be said therefore that among those that believed education to be included within the concept of civil equality there was unanimity in support of either segregation or integration.

CONCLUSIONS OF THE THESIS

The majority of those in Congress in 1866 either did not believe the Fourteenth Amendment was related to the question of Negro education or did not consider the possibility of their being related. A minority of those men in Congress in 1866, however, did believe Negro education to be within the scope of section one of the Amendment. The Amendment was further conceded by both Republicans and Democrats to be a change in the balance of power between state and federal authority. The inclusion of education in Sumner's civil rights bill of 1872, therefore, while not expressing popular thought, did represent ideas current at the time of the framing of the Fourteenth Amendment.

This fact is substantiated by thought and practice at the state level. State legislators, at the time of ratification, generally either believed the Amendment not related to Negro education or did not even consider the question. A minority opinion, on the other hand, did believe that Negro education was included either within the scope of section one of the Fourteenth Amendment *per se* or within the general concept of equality before the law. It was within the state departments of education, however, throughout the reconstruction period, that considerable expression was given to the belief that Negro education was included at least within the general concept of equality before the law. Some superintendents, in fact, referred specifically to the Fourteenth Amendment as the measure requiring equality in the provision for Negro and white education.

As for the integration issue itself, there was again divided thought at federal and state levels. Neither segregation nor integration, therefore, can unequivocally be associated with the Fourteenth Amendment. Most men in Congress throughout Reconstruction believed segregation in the schools an adequate and acceptable practice, and some referred to the separate but equal doctrine as an adequate guarantee of equality. A minority led by Sumner, on the other hand, felt integration necessary if there was to be an equality before the law. Many superintendents of education also believed segregation a satisfactory fulfillment of equality before the law, and some also referred to the separate but equal doctrine. Others, however, believed only integration could bring Negro and white upon a true level of equality.

BIBLIOGRAPHY

I. Manuscript Collections:

Bingham, John A. Ohio State Historical and. Archeological Society. This collection is of no value for a study of the Fourteenth Amendment. In the Joshua Reed Giddings papers (Ohio State Historical and Archeological Society), however, there are letters from Bingham dated before the War that shed light on his attitude toward slavery.

Carpenter, Matthew Hale. Wisconsin Historical Society. This collection, too, is of no value for a study of the Fourteenth Amendment. There are Carpenter letters, however, in the Charles D. Robinson papers (Wisconsin Historical Society). These are dated between 1863 and 1865 and indicate the nature of Carpenter's political persuasion at this time. (Robinson was editor of the Green Bay Advocate during these years.)

II. Published Letters and Speeches:

Boutwell, George S. Speeches and Papers Relating to the Rebellion and the Overthrow of Slavery. Boston, 1867.

Carpenter Matthew H. Writings of Matthew Hale Carpenter. 1865-1870. Bound pamphlets, Wisconsin Historical Society.

Conkling, Alfred R. The Life and Letters of Roscoe Conkling. New York, 1889.

Marshall, Jessie Ames, ed. Private and Official Correspondence of Gen. Benjamin F. Butler During the Period of the Civil War. 5 vols., Norwood (Massachusetts), 1917.

Pierce, Edward L., ed. Memoir and Letters of Charles Sumner. 4 vols., Boston, 1877, 1891.

Sumner, Charles. The Works of Charles Sumner, ed. by Francis V. Balch, Boston, 1874-1883.

Thorndike Rachel Sherman, ed. The Sherman Letters. New York, 1894. This volume contains correspondence between General and Senator Sherman from 1837 to 1891.

III. Memoirs:
Blaine, James G. Twenty Years of Congress: From Lincoln to Garfield. 2 vols., Norwich (Connecticut), 1893.

Boutwell, George S. Reminiscences of Sixty Years in Public Affairs. 2 vols., New York, 1902.

Butler, Benjamin F., Butler's Book. Boston, 1892. This book is not very helpful for a study of civil rights.

Cole, Cornelius. Memoirs of Cornelius Cole, Ex-Senator of the United States from California. New York, 1908.

Grinnell, Josiah B. Men and Events of Forty Years. Boston, 1891.

Hoar, George P. <u>Autobiography of Seventy Years</u>. 2 vols., New York, 1903. This work contains sketches of the political lives of Benjamin Butler, Charles Sumner, and. Henry Wilson, as well as documents about Negro education during the re-construction period.

Sherman, John. <u>John Sherman's Recollections of Forty Years in the House, Senate and Cabinet</u>. 2 vols., Chicago, 1895.

Stewart, William M. <u>Reminiscences of Senator William Stewart of Nevada</u>, ed. by George Roghwell Brown, New York, 1908.

IV. Government Documents:
<u>Alabama</u>:

<u>Annual Report of the Superintendent of Education of the State of Alabama. 1857. Montgomery, 1557.</u>

<u>Annual Report of the Superintendent of Public Instruction of the State of Alabama, 1874, 1876, 2 vols., Montgomery, 1874, 1876.</u>

<u>"Report of the Superintendent of Public Instruction of the State of Alabama," 1869 1871, 1873. State Documents. 3 vols., Montgomery, 1869, 1871, 1873.</u>

<u>Arkansas</u>:

<u>Acts of the General Assembly of the State of Arkansas, 1873. Little Rock, 1873.</u>

<u>Biennial Report of the Superintendent of Public Instruction, 1868-1870. Little Rock, 1870.</u>

Debates and Prooeedings of the Convention Which Assembled at Little Rock January 7 1868... to Form a Constitution for the State of Arkansas. Little Rock, 1865.

"Governor's Message," 1867. State Documents. Little Rock, 1867.

Journal of the House of Representatives, 1866-1867. Little Rock, 1870.

Journal of the Assembly of the State of Arkansas at Their Seventeenth Session, 1868-1869. 2 vols., Little Rock, 1868, 1870.

Journal of the Senate of Arkansas, 1866-1867, 1868-1869. 2 vols., Little Rock, 1869, 1870.

California:
Appendix to Journals of Senate and Assembly of the State of California, 1864-1875. 7 vols., Sacramento, 1866 1875.

Journal of the Assembly During the Seventeenth Session of the Legislature of the State of California 1867-8. Sacramento, 1868.

Journal of the Senate During the Nineteenth Session of the Legislature of the State of California, 1871-72. Sacramento, 1872.

Reports of Cases Determined in the Supreme Court of the State of California, at the January, April, July and October Terms, 1874. San Francisco, 1875.

School Law, 1864, 1866, 1873. 3 vols., Sacramento, 1864, 1866, 1873.

Congress:
  Congressional Globe.
    34 Cong., 3 sess., 1857.

  Congressional Globe.
    35 Cong., 2 sess., 1859.
    38 Cong., 1 sess. - 42 Cong., 3 sess., 1863-1873.

  Congressional Record.
    43 Cong., December, 1873 March, 1875.

  Reports of the Committees of the House of Representatives 1870-'71.

  Reports of the Committees of the Senate of the United States for the Second Session of the Forty-Second Congress 1871-'72.

  Report of the Joint Committee on Reconstruction, 1866.

Connecticut:
  "Annual Report of the Board of Education of the State of Connecticut, Public Documents of the Legislature of Connecticut, 1865-1871. 7 vols., Hartford and New Haven, '65-'71.

  "Governor's Message," Public Documents of the Legislature of Connecticut, 1867. Hartford, 1867.

Public Acts, Passed by the General Assembly of the State of Connecticut in the Years 1866, 1867, and 1868. Hartford, 1868.

Delaware:
First Annual Report of the Superintendent of Free Schools of the State of Delaware, 1876. Dover, 1877.

District of Columbia:
First Report of the Board of Trustees of Public Schools of the District of Columbia, 1874-'75. Washington, 1877.

Florida:
"Governor's Message," A Journalof the Proceedings of the House of Representatives of the General Assembly of the State of Florida, 1866. Tallahassee, 1866.

"Report of the Superintendent of Public Instruction of the State of Florida." A Journal of the Proceedings of the Assembly of the State of Florida, 1871, 1873. 2 vols., Tallahassee, 1872, 1874.

Freedmen's Bureau:
Semi-Annual Report on Schools for Freedmen, 1866-1870. 9 vols., Washington, 1868-1870.

Georgia:
First Annual Report of the State School Commissioner of the State of Georgia, 1871. Atlanta, 1871.

"Governor's Message," Journal of' the House of Representatives of the State of Georgia, 1866, 1868. 2 vols., Milledgeville and Macon, 1866, 1868.

Journal of the Proceedings of the Constitutional Convention of the People of Georgia, 1868. Augusta, 1868.

Illinois:
"Biennial Report of the Superintendent of Public Instruction of the State of Illinois," Reports Made to the General Assembly of Illinois, 1867-1868, 1869-1870, 1871-1872. 3 vols., Springfield, 1869, 1871, 1873.

Biennial Report of the Superintendent of Public Instruction of the State of Illinois, 1872-1874. (No publication data.)

"Governors Message," Reports Made to the General Assembly of Illinois, 1867. Springfield, 1867.

Journal of the Constitutional Convention of the State of Illinois, 1870. Springfield, 1870.

Indiana:
"Governor's Message," Documents of the General Assembly of Indiana, 1867. Indianapolis, 1867.

Report of the Superintendent of Public Instruction for the State of Indiana, 1863-1872, 1875. 6 vols., Indianapolis, 1865-1872, 1875.

"Report of the Superintendent of Public Instruction of the State of Indiana," 1873, 1874. 2 vols., Indianapolis, 1874, 1875.

Reports of Cases Argued and Determined in the Supreme Court of Judicature of the State of Indiana, 1874. Indianapolis, 1891.

Iowa:

"Biennial Report of the Superintendent of Public Instruction," Legislative Documents...of the State of Iowa, 1865-1876. 6 vols., Des Moines, 1866-1876.

"Governor's Message," Legislative Documents...of the State of Iowa, 1868. Des Moines, 1868.

Reports of Cases in Law and Equity, Determined in the Supreme Court of the State of Iowa, vol. XXIV, Des Moines, 1877.

Kansas:

"Annual Message of Gov. James M. Harvey, Delivered to the Kansas Legislature, January, 1869," State Documents. (No publication data.)

Annual Report of the Superintendent of Public Instruction of the State of Kansas, 1865-1875. 11 vols., Leavenworth and Topeka, 1866-1876.

Laws of the State of Kansas Passed, at the Fourteenth Session of the Legislature, 1874. Topeka, 1874.

Proceedings of the Legislative Assembly of the State of Kansas, 1873, 1874. 4 vols., Topeka, 1873, 1874.

Kentucky:

Annual Report of the Superintendent of Public Instruction of Kentucky, 1865-1868. 4 vols., Frankfort, 1866-1869.

"Annual Report of the Superintendent of Public Instruction of Kentucky," State Documents, 1870-1875. 5 vols., Frankfort, 1871-1875.

Journal of the Senate of the Commonwealth of Kentucky, 1865-1866, 1866-1867. 2 vols., Frankfort, 1867.

Louisiana:
"Annual Report of the Superintendent of Public Education ...of Louisiana," Documents of the Legislature of the State of Louisiana, 1866-1875, 1877. 9 vols., New Orleans, 1866-1576, 1878.

"Message of Governor R.C. Warmoth, Vetoing the Civil Rights Bill," Documents..., 1867-1868. New Orleans, 1868.

Maine:
Annual Report of the Superintendent of Common Schools of the State of Maine, 1866-1868. 3 vols., Augusta, 1866-1868.

Maryland:
"Governor's Message," Public Documents of the House of Delegates of Maryland, 1868. Annapolis, 1868.

Journal of the Proceedings of the Senate of Maryland, 1867.-Annapolis, 1867.

Proceedings of the State Convention of Maryland to Frame a New Constitution, 1867.-Annapolis, 1867.

Report of the State Board of Education...of Maryland, 1866, 1868, 1871, 1872, 1874. 5 vols., Annapolis, 1867, 1869, 1872, 1873, 1875.

"Report of the Principal of the State Normal School Shewing the Condition of the Public Schools of Maryland," State Documents, 1869.-Annapolis, 1870.

Massachusetts:

"Annual Report of the Board of Education," Public Documents of Massachusetts, 1865-1872. 8 vols., Boston, 1866-1873.

Documents printed by Order of the House of Representatives of the Commonwealth of Massachusetts, 1867. Boston, 1867.

"Governor's Message," Documents Printed by Order of the Senate of the Commonwealth of Massachusetts, 1867. Boston, 1867.

Michigan:

Acts of the Legislature of the State of Michigan, 1867. 2 vols., Lansing, 1867.

"Annual Report of the Superintendent of Public Instruction of the State of Michigan," Joint Documents of the State of Michigan, 1865-1875. 11 vols., Lansing, 1865-1876.

Debates and. Proceedings of the Constitutional Convention of the State of Michigan, 1867. 2 vols., Lansing, 1867.

Reports of Cases Heard and Decided in the Supreme Court of Michigan from January 11, 1869, to July 12, 1869. Chicago, 1879.

Minnesota:

Annual Report of the Secretary of State and Superintendent of Public Instruction, to the Legislature of Minnesota, 1866. Saint Paul, 1867.

Annual Report of the Superintendent of Public Instruction for the State of Minnesota, 1867, 1873. 2 vols., Saint Paul, 1868, 1874.

"Annual Report of the Superintendent of Public Instruction for the State of Minnesota," Executive Documents of the State of Minnesota, 1868-1871, 1874-1875. 6 vols., Saint Paul, 1869-1872, 1875-1876.

"Governor's Message," Executive Documents…, 1867. Saint Paul, 1868.

Mississippi:
 "Annual Report of the Superintendent of Public Education, State Documents, 1871. (No publication data.)

Annual Report of the Superintendent of Public Education for the State of Mississippi, 1872, 1874, 1875. 3 vols., Jackson, 1873, 1875, 1876.

"Governor's Message," Journal of the Senate of the State of Mississippi, 1866, 1870. 2 vols., Jackson, 1866, 1870.

Missouri:
 Appendix to the Senate Journal of the Adjourned Session of the Twenty-Third General Assembly of the State of Missouri, 1865. Jefferson City, 1865-6.

Appendix to the House and Senate Journals of the Regular Session of the Twenty-Fifth General Assembly…, 1869. Jefferson City, 1869.

"Governor's Message," Journal of the Missouri State Senate, 1867. Jefferson City, 1869.

Laws of the State of Missouri, 1865, 1866. 2 vols., Jefferson City, 1865, 1866.

Nebraska:
Annual Report of the State Superintendent of Public Instruction, 1869-1874. 6 vols., Omaha, Des Moines, and Lincoln, 1869-1874.

"Governor's Message," Senate Journal of the State Legislature of Nebraska, 1867. Omaha, 1867.

School Laws of Nebraska. Des Moines, 1871.

Nevada:
"Biennial Report of the Superintendent of Public Instruction of the State of Nevada," 1865-1866, 1869-1870. Journal of the Senate, 1867, 1871. 2 vols., Carson City, 1867, 1871.

"Fourth Annual Report of the Superintendent of Public Instruction of the State of Nevada,'" 1868, Journal of the Senate, 1869. Carson City, 1869.

"Governor's Message," Journal of the Senate, 1867. Carson City, 1867.

New Hampshire:
Annual Report Upon the Common Schools of New Hampshire, 1866-1868. 3 vols., Concord and Manchester, 1866-1868.

"Governor's Message," Journal of the House of Representatives of the State of New Hampshire, 1867. Manchester, 1867.

New Jersey:
"Annual Report of the State Superintendent of Public Instruction of the State of New Jersey," 1865-1874 Documents of the Legislature of the State of New Jersey, 1866-1875. 10 vols., New Brunswick, et. al., 1866-1875.

"Governor's Message," Documents..., 1867. Jersey City, 1868.

New York:
"Annual Report of the Superintendent of Public Instruction of the State of New York," 1865-1870, 1872-1873, Documents of the Assembly of the State of New York, 1866-1871, 1873-1874. 8 vols., Albany, 1866-1871, 1873-1874.

"Governor's Message," Documents..., 1867. Albany, 1867.

Journal of the Assembly of the State of New York, 1873. 2 vols., Albany, 1873.

Journal of the Senate of the State of New York, 1873, Albany, 1873.

Proceedings and Debates of the Constitutional Convention of the State of New York, 1867-1868. 5 vols., Albany, 1868.

North Carolina:
"Governor's Message," Executive and Legislative Documents...of North Carolina, 1866-1867. Raleigh, 1867.

Journal of the Constitutional Convention of the State of North Carolina, 1868. Raleigh, 1868.

"Report of Superintendent of Public Instruction" 1869-1874, Executive and Legislative Documents..., 6 vols., Raleigh, 1570-1575.

Ohio:

Annual Report of the State Commissioner of Common Schools," Annual Reports, 1863-1864, 1866-1875. 12 vol., Columbus, 1864-1865, 1867-1876.

"Governor's Message," Annual Reports, 1867. Columbus, 1868.

Official Report of the Proceedings and Debates of the Third Constitutional Convention of Ohio. 2 vols., Cleveland, 1873.

Reports of Cases Argued and Determined in the Supreme Court of Ohio, vol. XXI, Cincinnati, 1873.

Oregon:

"Governor's Message," Journal of the Proceedings of the House of the Legislative Assembly of Oregon. 1866. Salem, 1866.

"Inaugural Address of Gov. L.F. Grover," State Documents, 1870. Salem, 1870.

"Report of the Superintendent of Public Instruction," State Documents, 1874. Salem, 1874.

Pennsylvania:

Debates of the Convention to Amend the Constitution of Pennsylvania, 1872-1873 8 vols., Harrisburg, 1873.

"Governor's Message," Journal of the House of Representatives of the Commonwealth of Pennsylvania. 1867. Harrisburg, 1867.

Journal of the Senate of the Commonwealth of Pennsylvania, 1867. Harrisburg, 1867.

"Report of the Superintendent of Common Schools, of the Commonwealth of Pennsylvania," 1865-1873. 9 vols., Harrisburg, 1866-1874.

Rhode Island:
Annual Report on Public Schools in Rhode Island, 1867, 1868, 1870. 3 vols., Providence, 1867, 1686, 1870.

South Carolina:
"Annual Report of the Superintendent of Education of the State of South Carolina," 1868-1875, Reports and Resolutions of the General Assembly, 1868-1376. 7 vols., Columbia, 1868-1876.

Journal of the House of Representatives of the State of South Carolina, 1866. Columbia, 1866.

Proceedings of the Constitutional Convention of South Carolina, 1865. Charleston, 1865.

Reports and Resolutions of the General Assembly of the State of South Carolina, 1866. Columbia, 1866.

Tennessee:
Annual Report of the Superintendent of Public Instruction of the State of Tennessee, 1869, 1875. 2 vols., Nashville, 1869, 1876.

"Annual Report of John M. Fleming, State Superintendent of Public Instruction for Tennessee," 1874 Appendix to the Journal of the House of Representatives, 1874. Nashville, 1875.

House Journal of the Called Session of the General Assembly of the State of Tennessee, 1866. Nashville, 1866.

Senate Journal of the Called Session of the General Assembly of the State of Tennessee, 1866. Nashville, 1866.

Texas:

Annual Report of the Superintendent of Public Instruction of the State of Texas, 1871, 1872, 1874. 3 vols., Austin, and Houston, 1872, 1873, 1874.

General Laws of the Twelfth Legislature of the State of Texas. Austin, 1870.

General Laws of the State of Texas. Austin, 1873.

"Governor's Message," Journal of the House of Representatives, 1866. Austin, 1866.

Journal of the Senate of Texas, 1866. Austin, 1866.

Vermont:

Annual Report of the Vermont Board of Education, 1867, 1868. 2 vols., Burlington and. Montpelier, 1867, 1868.

"Governor's Report," Vermont Legislative Documents and Official Reports, 1866. Montpelier, 1866.

Virginia:

"Annual Report of the Superintendent of Public Instruction," 1870-1875. Annual Reports, 1870-1875. 6 vols., Richmond, 1870-1875.

Debates and. Proceedings of the Constitutional Convention of the State of Virginia, 1868, vol., Richmond, 1865.

"Governor's Message," Journal of the House of Delegates of the State of Virginia, 1874. Richmond, 1874.

Journal of the Senate of the Commonwealth of Virginia, 1866. Richmond, 1866.

West Virginia:

Annual Report of the General Superintendent of Public Schools, 1869. Wheeling, 1870.

"Annual Report of the General Superintendent of Public Schools, of the State of West Virginia," 1868, Journal of the House of Delegates of the State of West Virginia, 1869. Wheeling, 1869.

"Annual Report of the General Superintendent of Public Schools, of the State of West Virginia," 1870, 1871, State Documents, 1870, 1871. (No publication data.)

Journal of Constitutional Convention, 1872. Charleston, 1872.

Wisconsin:

"Annual Report of the Superintendent of Public Instruction of the State of Wisconsin," 1865-1866, Governor's Message and Accompanying Documents of the State of Wisconsin, 1867. Madison, 1867.

"Annual Report of the Superintendent of Public Instruction of the State of Wisconsin," 1867, State Documents, 1867. Madison, 1867.

Annual Report of the Superintendent of Public Instruction of the State of Wisconsin, 1868-1875. 8 vols., Madison, 1868-1875.

"Governor's Message," State Documents, 1867. Madison, 1867.

Journal of the Senate of Wisconsin, 1867. Madison, 1867.

V. Newspapers;
Atchison Daily Champion.
Boston Daily Advertiser.
Chicago Tribune.
Cincinnati Daily Inquirer.
Columbus Daily Enquirer (Georgia).
Crisis (Columbus, Ohio).
Daily Memphis Avalanche.
Daily Milwaukee News.
Daily Picayune.
Daily Richmond Examiner.
Elevator (San Francisco, Negro).
Evening Bulletin (San Francisco).
Evening Post (New York).
Louisianian (New Orleans, Negro).
Morning Oregonian (Portland).
New Orleans Tribune (Negro).

<u>New York Times.</u>
<u>Philadelphia Inquirer.</u>
<u>Public Ledger (Philadelphia).</u>
<u>Sacramento Daily Union.</u>
<u>Saint Paul Pioneer.</u>
<u>Southern Recorder (Milledgeville, Georgia).</u>
<u>Springfield Weekly Republican (Massachusetts).</u>
<u>Sun (Baltimore).</u>
<u>Wisconsin State Journal (Madison).</u>

VI. <u>Biography</u>:

Few of the biographical works of men of this period are really significant for this particular study. The following materials are helpful, however, for an understanding of the personalities involved.

"Allen G. Thurman." <u>The Nation</u>, XLVI (June 14 1888), 480-481. There is reference in this article to Thurman's interpretation of the Fourteenth Amendment, which he had argued in Congress in the 1870's.

Brown, Ernest Francis. <u>Raymond of the Times</u>. New York, 1951.

Chidsey, Donald Barr. <u>The Gentleman from New York: A Life of Roscoe Conkling</u>. Yale University Press, 1935.

Current, Richard Nelson. <u>Old Thad Stevens. A Story of Ambition</u>. The University of Wisconsin Press, 1942.

Fessenden, Francis. Life and Public Services of William Pitt Fessenden. 2 vols., Boston, 1907.

Flower, Frank A. Life of Matthew Hale Carpenter. Madison, 1883.

Roar, George P. "Charles Sumner " The North American Review cxxvi (January 1878), 1-6. This article refers to Sumner's efforts for the guarantee of Negro civil rights and the provision for Negro education.

Hogue, Arthur Reed, ed. (<u>Charles Sumner. An Essay by Carl Schurz</u>. The University of Illinois Press, 1951. The essay was written about 1894 and was based primarily on Pierce, Edward L. <u>Memoir and Letters of Charles Sumner</u>. 4 vols., Boston, 1877, 1894.

Holzman, Robert S. <u>Stormy Ben Butler</u>. New York, 1954.

Korngold., Ralph. <u>Thaddeus Stevens: A Being Darkly Wise and Rudely Great</u>. New York, 1955.

"Letters to Prominent Persons," <u>The North American Review</u>, CXLII (May 1886), 441-451. There is some discussion of Reconstruction legislation. The article is about Thurman.

Randall, James O. "John Sherman and Reconstruction," <u>Mississippi Valley Historical Review</u>, XIX (December 1932), This article, originally an address before the Mississippi Valley Historical Association, April 24, 1930, emphasizes Sherman's role as a moderate within the Republican party--a moderate, however, who eventually identified himself with the Radicals.

Salter, William. <u>The Life of James W. Grimes</u>. New York, 1876

Shotwell, Walter Gaston. <u>Driftwood</u>. New York, 1927. This book is a general, non-critical biography of Bingham.

Steiner, Bernard C. Life of Reverdy Johnson, Baltimore, 1914.

"Thaddeus Stevens." The Nation, VII (August 20, 1868), 145 146.

Thompson, E. Bruce. Matthew Hale Carpenter, Webster of the West. Madison, 1954.

Trefousse, Hans L. Ben Butler, New York, 1957

Webb, Richard, "William Pitt Fessenden." New England Magazine, 18 (March 1898), 116-129.

White, Horace. The Life of Lyman Trumbull. Boston, 1913. This work relies heavily upon the Congressional Globe as a reference for his life during the reconstruction period.

Whitridge, Frederick W., "Roscoe Conkling." International Review, XI (October 1881), 375-390. This article is a critical review of his public life and legal career.

VII.   General Works:
Fourteenth Amendment:

Bickel., Alexander M., The Original Understanding and the Segregation Decision." Harvard Law Review, 69 (November 1955), 1-65. Bickel believes that "civil rights" included education in 1866 but did not mean that schools were to be integrated.

Bond, Horace Mann. "The Educational Significance and Impact of the Fourteenth Amendment on Constitutional and Statutory Provisions for Segregated and Non-Segregated Education of Negroes in the United States (With Especial Reference to the Period. 1866-1875 Immediately Subsequent to the Submission of the Amendment on June 20, 1866)." Unpublished material prepared as an appendix to the appellant's brief in the case of Brown v. The Board of Education (347 U.S. 483). Howard. K. Beale papers.

Fairman, Charles. "Does the Fourteenth Amendment Incorporate the Bill of Rights? The Original Understanding." Stanford Law Review, 2 (December 1949), 5-139. This study is based upon the debates in congress, and Fairman reaches the conclusion that there was no clear conception at the time of the framing of the Fourteenth Amendment of the meaning of the first section, particularly the privileges and immunities clause.

Flack, Horace E. The Adoption of the Fourteenth Amendment. The Johns Hopkins Press, 1908. This work is a history of the framing of the Fourteenth Amendment.

Frank, John P. and Robert P. Munro. "The Original Understanding of 'Equal Protection of the Laws.'" Columbia Law Review, 50 (February 1950), 131-169. This study notes the differences of opinion among those men who were members of the Joint Committee of Fifteen with regard to the meaning of 'equal protection of the laws." The phrase was meant to include transportation, hotels, and theaters, the authors conclude, but there was a difference of opinion about the school issue. This study contains a review of congressional debate on civil rights for the ten year period, 1866-1875.

Graham, Howard Jay. "The Purpose and Meaning of Section One and Five of the Fourteenth Amendment. The Historical Evidence Reexamined." Unpublished material prepared as an appendix to the appellant's brief in the case of Brown v. Board of Education. This study is a discussion of the constitutional background of section one of the Fourteenth Amendment and also a history of abolitionist argument up to 1866. Howard K. Beale papers.

James, Joseph B. <u>The Framing of the Fourteenth Amendment</u>. The University of Illinois Press, 1956. This critical study does not include within its scope the question of school segregation.

Kelly, Alfred H. "Congress, the Fourteenth Amendment, and School Segregation Statutes." Unpublished material prepared as an appendix to the appellant's brief in the case of Brown v. Board of Education. Howard K. Beale papers.

Kelly, Alfred H. "The Fourteenth Amendment Reconsidered: The Segregation Question." <u>Michigan Law Review</u>, 54 (June 1956), 1049-1086. Kelly believes that Bingham was a Radical intending, with Stevens, to enlarge the scope of the Civil Rights Act by constitutional amendment. The Fourteenth Amendment was as comprehensive in scope, Kelly maintains, as the Democratic opposition indicated at the time.

Kendrick, Benjamin B. <u>The Journal of the Joint Committee of Fifteen on Reconstruction.</u> Columbia University Press, 1911.. This volume is a record of proposals considered by the Committee, together with a record of votes taken on those proposals. (There is no record of the Committee debates.)

Leyland, Herbert Thompson. <u>The Concept of Due Process of Law in 1866 and Its Influence on the Fourteenth Amendment</u>. The University of Wisconsin press, 1922. This study is based upon the <u>Congressional Globe</u>, Flack, and Kendrick.

McLaughlin, Andrew C. "The Court, the Corporation, and Conkling." <u>American Historical Review</u>, XLVI (October 1940), 45-63. This article is a discussion of the meaning of "person" in the Fourteenth Amendment. His conclusion is that "person" was not meant to include the corporation.

Morrison, Stanley. "Does the Fourteenth Amendment incorporate the Bill of Rights? The Judicial Interpretation." Stanford Law Review, 2 (December 1949), 140-173. The conclusion of this study is that the Amendment does not incorporate the Bill of Rights.

Owen, Robert Dale. "Practical Results from the Varioloid." Atlantic Monthly, XXXV (June 1875), 660-670.

Steiner, Bernard C. "History of Slavery in Connecticut,'" vol. 11, <u>Johns Hopkins University Studies in History and Political Science</u>, ed. by Herbert B. Adams. Johns Hopkins Press, 1893.

ten Broek, Jacobus. <u>The Antislavery Origins of the Fourteenth Amendment</u>. The University of California Press, 1951.

"The 39th Congress Contemplated and Understood that the Fourteenth Amendment Would Make Unlawful Any and All. State Laws Based on a Difference in Race, Including Compulsory School Segregation Laws." Unpublished material prepared as an appendix to the appellant's brief in the case of Brown v. Board of Education. (Author's name not given.) Howard K. Beale papers.

Negro Education:

Blum, Albert. Summary of State's Reports. Unpublished material prepared as an appendix to the appellant's brief in the case of Brown v. Board of Education. This study reviews changes that occurred in legislation during Reconstruction with regard to the segregation issue. Howard K. Beale papers.

Bond, Horace Mann. The Education of the Negro in the American Social Order. New York, 1934.

Franklin, John Hope. "The Genesis of Segregation in the New South with Special Reference to Separate Schools for Negroes. Unpublished material prepared as an appendix to the appellant's brief in the case of Brown v. Board of Education. Howard K. Beale papers.

Swint, Henry Lee. The Northern Teacher in the South. Vanderbilt University Press, 1941.

Taylor, Alrutheus A. the Negro in the Reconstruction of Virginia. Washington, 1926. This book, one of a series for the Association for the Study of Negro life and History, contains a chapter on education. One other book in this series by Taylor is The Negro in South Carolina During

Reconstruction (Washington, 192⁴), which also has a chapter on education.

Reconstruction:

Barnes, William H. <u>History of the Thirty-Ninth Congress of the United States</u>. New York, 1868.

Beale, Howard K. <u>The Critical Year</u>. New York, 1930.

Bentley, George R. <u>A History of the Freedmen's Bureau</u>. The University of Pennsylvania Press, 1955.

Blaine, James G. <u>Political Discussions Legislative, Diplomatic, and Popular 1856-1886</u>. Norwich (Connecticut), 1887.

Boutwell, George S. <u>The Constitution of the United States at the End of the First Century</u>. Boston, 1895.

Boutwell, George S. "General Grant's Administration," <u>McClure's Magazine</u>, XIV (February 1900), 355-362.

Bowers, Claude G. <u>The Tragic Era</u>. Cambridge, 1929.

Ficklen, John Rose. <u>History of Reconstruction in Louisiana</u>. The John Hopkins Press, 1910.

Fleming, Walter L. <u>Civil War and Reconstruction in Alabama</u>. Columbia University Press, 1905.

Fleming, Walter L. Documentary History of Reconstruction, New edition. 2 vols. New York, 1950.

Knight, Edgar W. Influence of Reconstruction on Education. Columbia University Press, 1913.

Lynch, John R. The Facts of Reconstruction. New York, 1913.

Simpkins, Francis Butler, and Robert Hilliard Woody. South Carolina During Reconstruction. The University of North Carolina Press, 1932.

Thorpe, Francis Newton. The Federal and State Constitutions. 7 vols. Washington, 1909.

Wharton, Vernon Lane. The Negro in Mississippi, 1865-1890. The University of North Carolina Press, 1947.

ABOUT THE AUTHOR

Robert Stuart lives in East Hampton, New York. From the Midwest, he graduated from Webster Groves High School, Webster Groves, Missouri. He received his bachelor's degree from DePauw University and master's degrees from the University of Wisconsin and Princeton Theological Seminary. He is a Presbyterian minister.

Stuart is a member of the Ashawagh Hall Writers Workshop, East Hampton. He initially wrote *The Fourteenth Amendment and Its Intent for Education* after the controversial *Brown v. Board of Education* decision.